T0129375

LEADERSHIP REFLECTIONS

A Leader's Personal Journey

DR. WRIGHT L. LASSITER, JR.

Order this book online at www.trafford.com
or email orders@trafford.com

Most Trafford titles are also available at major online book retailers.

Printed in the United States of America.

ISBN: 978-1-4907-4037-9 (sc)
ISBN: 978-1-4907-4036-2 (hc)
ISBN: 978-1-4907-4035-5 (e)

Library of Congress Control Number: 2014911268

Trafford rev. 06/23/2014

North America & international
toll-free: 1 888 232 4444 (USA & Canada)
fax: 812 355 4082

CONTENTS

Introduction ix
Foreword xiii
The Power of Words xvii
Acknowledgments and Dedication xix

PART ONE

The Life Story in Abstract

A Gift of the River 3
Plan Your Legacy Early 5
Career Interview... 9
The Alcorn Experience 12
DCCCD First African American Chancellor 16
The Role of the Chancellor... 18
The "Largest Room" Context 21
Focus on Cultural Differences Interview 25
Let Your Life Speak.. 29
Nothing Much Happens Without a Dream 35
Dare to Follow Your Dreams... 39

PART TWO

Lessons in Leadership

Leadership Expressions of Wright Lassiter............................... 47
The "How-To-Be" Leader Going Forward 49
Mentoring Guidance.. 52

Thoughts on Adversity and Opportunity.. 55
The Hardest Person to Lead 56
How to Deal With Failure 59
Nine Truths of Community College Leadership 62
Forty Lessons Learned Over Four Decades 64
Appreciation Aids Motivation 67

PART THREE

The Servant Leader

The Purpose of Life 73
My Life Is Not My Own.. 75
Questions I Ask Myself 78
Perspectives on Servant Leadership... 80
Who Is the Servant Leader?... 83
The Serving Leader 86
Ten Characteristics of a Servant Leader.. 88
A Servant Leader's Journey: Experiences and Influences.................... 90
Relationships Are A Measure of Stewardship.................................... 98
The Role of Personal Leadership... 100
Leadership Is About the People for Whom We Are Responsible........103

PART FOUR

The Path to the Presidency

Have You Heard the Call?.. 107
The Search Process 109
Five Reasons to Aspire to the Presidency 111
Stepping Through the Leadership Door as a College President..........113
The Presidency as a Journey: Not a Destination 117
The Anatomy of a New President 119
Essential Principles for New Presidents... 120
Successful Presidents Court Risk and Change..................................121
Presidential Relationships: Build Them with Caution...................... 123
Reflections after Three Decades of CEO Service on the
Business of Leading a College 126

The College President of the Future Reflections of a Founder............ 130
Emerging From Within—How to Do It 133
Keys for Well-Rounded Leadership 136
The Leader's Covenant 138

PART FIVE

End Notes

Concluding Personal Reflections on Leadership 143
About the Author and His Inspiration..147

INTRODUCTION

A leader's voice can be quiet, dignified, bold, inspirational, demanding, angry, impatient, or a combination of several expressions. But underneath its variety, a deeper, more personal voice informs all the others. It is an essential voice that grows from the leader's unique identity and connects followers to his/her core values and beliefs. It is not easy to know since its essence is typically hidden beneath the varied expressions of the day-to-day, and since sharing from this quieter, deeper place is often a risk. There is also the possibility that once revealed, it may not be an appealing voice. But when a leader's voice is worthy and marches to a group's needs, it can offer confidence, hope, and trust.

Unfortunately, in a large organization such as the Dallas County Community College District, it is not easy to know the essential voice of the top leader. Most of us are not able to hear or observe often enough, over sufficient enough time, through the various seasons of organizational life to know the leader's style, tenor, and character. Yet I believe it is precisely this voice that Chancellor Wright Lassiter has carefully crafted for the nearly eight years of his tenure as the district chief executive officer. He produced volumes I and II of *The Essential Voice* that were distributed internally to all employees. He then wrote two books that received wide acclaim—*The Words of a College President* and *The Friday Messages: Food for Thought*. The contents of the books were products from his weekly Friday Commentary, which made it possible for the district community to "hear and feel" their leader.

The chancellor loves to write. The words and ideas that appear in this twelfth volume grow from his own personal generative effort. They are typically written in the quiet of his home library/study and are the result of disciplined, contemplative thought. In writing to the DCCCD community, his tone is respectfully personal—as if Dr. Lassiter is writing a letter to a colleague he admires. Rather than remaining detached, he intentionally shows us what he cares about through his words.

He generously shares his words. We have come to expect the "Friday Message" that is not just informative, but personal and reflective. In my experience, his willingness to share in this way is unprecedented. He also reinforces the written word with frequent "road shows," where he speaks to district locations and gatherings, providing a remarkable consistent point of view as he shifts from writing to speaking. Many of his invitations to appear and speak come from student organizations at the seven colleges of the district. These invitations are generally always accepted unless there is a major schedule conflict.

He is a lifelong learner with a scholarly bent who has never tired of mining new resources. His pattern is to connect this constant study to his own experience and to the organization he serves. The varied, sometimes surprising resources he shares not only indicate his personal interests, but his leadership character and his perspective on leadership. He is an unquestioned exponent and model of servant leadership.

He speaks directly to us, not to some generalized audience. Ask him, and Dr. Lassiter will tell you that there is no organic link between what he chooses to write about and the experience of his week. He not only responds to what we say or do, but to his intuitive sense of our needs. His commentaries underscore his willingness to relate to us and to make a personal connection. One of his oft-used phrases is "food for thought."

When he speaks, Dr. Lassiter eagerly shares his hopes and dreams for the organization. It is difficult not to know key elements of his vision for the DCCCD in his references to collaboration, communication, leadership, and values. At heart, he believes the strength of our community will determine our capacity to move from good to great. While some might be skeptical of such idealism, he is not—nor is he shy in its expression.

From time to time, he shares the lens of his personal faith. In a world of political correctness where most of us are guarded, his comments include references to the spiritual life that is fundamental to his makeup. It is a compliment that he trusts us in this way and that his manner honors rather than threatens our own beliefs.

For all these reasons, and because Wright Lassiter speaks with wisdom at a critical point in the Dallas County Community College District's history, I commend this volume to a potentially large array of readers. This is a critical point as this is a volume written shortly after his retirement as chancellor, and in his new role as chancellor emeritus. It is his hope that through the words, there is an expanded opportunity to continue to hear his essential voice. It is for the reader to determine how the future we hold as individuals, and as a community, can be strengthened by your perceptions of his words.

Nancy LeCroy, April 2014

FOREWORD

Reading, writing, and speaking have been foundations of my personal and professional life. Through the use of those skills, I have honed my capacity as a teacher, speaker, and leader. Hearing me speak, or teach, there would be individuals from the audience who could frequently ask for a copy of my talk. In the organizations where I served and worked, I would be frequently asked, "Why don't you write a book sometime?" My general response would be simple: "Thank you for your kind remarks regarding my presentation. Perhaps at some point in the future, I will be inspired to write a book and follow your suggestion."

One of my colleagues at Tuskegee Institute, where my journey began and had its roots, was Dr. William R. Harvey, the longtime and current president of Hampton University. As both of us as that time in our careers were aspiring to higher office, there was an occasion when we remarked to each other that we should carefully retain and catalog the full manuscripts of our speeches and other presentations. I have meticulously followed that practice, and it was in my third presidency at El Centro College that the "light went off," and I felt inspired to try my hand at writing a book.

As you read in Nancy LeCroy's introduction from that collection of speeches, presentations, and sermons, I have published eleven books and several monographs. The titles are presented in the final section of this book. With the exception of the published sermons, the books developed from my work as a coach/mentor to a large number of talented and motivated individuals who sought my advice and counsel. I was a faculty member for the Executive Leadership Institute of the League for Innovation in the community college where I provided counsel to individuals who were on the cusp of being prepared for service as a college president. For a number of years, I was a faculty member for the Institute for Academic Administrators sponsored by the College of Education at the University of Texas at Austin. I also served as a presenter for the President's Round Table, a unique assembly of African-American presidents/chancellors serving at community colleges in the nation. I also teach at the master's and doctoral levels at Dallas Baptist University where I have been accorded the title of Distinguished Adjunct Professor.

When I was elected the chancellor of the Dallas County Community College District after twenty years serving as the president of the flagship college in that system, El Centro College, one of my early challenges was to craft a new view of the role of the chief executive officer of the system. I concluded that communication had to be a major strategy.

To pursue that strategy, I began to write a weekly commentary that had the title of "The Largest Room Bulletin." One might ask, "How did you craft that title?" It is the product of one of my themes that I use in teaching, speaking, and leading: "The largest room in any house is the room for improvement." A short while later, it was restyled as the "Weekend Memo." In that restyled format, the Weekend Memo had my commentary as the opening section, followed by short updates from the seven colleges and the two district administrative locations. That change was warmly embraced to such an extent that I had to inform the location editors that the maximum number of location updates would be four. Our objective of an informed community was being realized through this communication vehicle.

This book is one of two books that will represent my last publications on leadership in higher education administration. The purpose of this book is to produce a literal "toolbox" of ideas, practices, and experiences that other aspiring executives could find useful and helpful in their career planning. The seasoned leader may find it helpful as they work to encourage, empower, and equip members of their staff.

My professional journey is chronicled with reflections and guidance resulting from my experiences as a higher education leader. It should be noted here that there have been twelve of my former colleagues who have advanced to the level of chief executive officer of a college or university. A parent always has a special place in his/her heart for the firstborn child. So it is with persons like myself who assist others in attaining a lofty goal. My first "child" was Dr. Curtis Ivery, the chancellor of the Wayne County Community College System in Detroit, Michigan. He, like the others, saw wisdom and merit in the manner in which I coached and guided them. As the firstborn holds a special place, so does the youngest "child." In the "Lassiter leadership family," the youngest is Dr. Toni Pendergrass, president of San Juan College (New Mexico).

One of the early messages in this book is the challenge and importance of legacy planning early in a career. I hold Curtis Ivery and Toni Hopper-Pendergrass up as two examples that put those principles into practice in their professional lives.

I describe the College Business Management Internship Program in some detail in the book. As a result of my experience in that program, I established an early goal in my life to aid others because of the manner in which I was trained. The time came when I was asked to serve as the leader/coach/teacher for the program. There were thirty-six individuals who came under my tutelage and graduated from the program. Several did become chief financial officers, others moved into senior positions, and a smaller number entered the corporate world and experienced success there.

I continually receive telephone calls and visits from individuals who want to come under "my wing" so to speak. Some who seek me out have been unsuccessful in their quests, and seek my advice on what to do to improve their chances. Others want guidance as they craft professional development experiences for their colleagues. As there are limits to personal encounters, it is my hope that this book will become a desk reference, as may be needed. As will be noted in various parts of the book, I try to give practical suggestions. As I conclude this foreword, the reader will note several factors that I consider pivotal. By placing a short summary here, the reader may be influenced to "read more."

Factors that are nonnegotiable

- Demonstrating consistent strong performance.
- Displaying ethics, integrity, and character.
- Being driven to lead and to assume higher levels of responsibility.

Factors leading to not being selected

- Weak interpersonal skills.
- Treating others with insensitivity or abrasiveness.
- Putting self-interest over the welfare of the organization.
- Holding a narrow, parochial perspective on the work of the organization

Factors that could lead to selection

- Displaying capabilities that breed confidence in others.
- Being able to set direction and think strategically.
- Being able to demonstrate the capacity to build a team.
- Managing implementation without getting unnecessarily bogged down in details.
- Showing the capacity for innovation.
- Having a tolerance to take risks and bring new ideas to fruition.
- Getting things done across boundaries (lateral management).
- Possessing the capacity to influence and persuade colleagues and deal effectively with conflict.
- Personal growth and development as an executive.

Over the years, I have gained a reputation for being a highly respected teacher, mentor, role model, and servant leader. As will be noted throughout this volume, teaching and aiding others has been a practice at every stage in my professional journey. Experiences and "words of wisdom" are presented in the four parts of the book:

- Part One—The Life Story in Abstract
- Part Two—Lessons in Leadership
- Part Three—The Servant Leader
- Part Four—Paths to the Presidency

THE POWER OF WORDS

It is through the careful and planned use of words that one communicates and practices what I call the "gift of persuasion." For three summers, I used a portion of my vacation time to accompany doctoral students at Dallas Baptist University to the nation's capital to spend a week studying historical and organizational leadership. That period of teaching was a form of renewal for me and the two other faculty members on the team. The two subjects that I focused on were organizational leadership and the leadership lessons of Dr. Martin Luther King Jr.

As an introduction to one of my lectures, I used three items tucked away in my files on the power of words. As words represent the common tool that we all use in our professional lives, you may find some utility in my thoughts shared with my students on the power of words.

Words are the instruments with which we build our world—our bridges to each other. I cannot see your thoughts directly. You must convey them to me clumsily or well. This is why we feel so frustrated when words fail us at important moments, when we feel we cannot reach another person despite our desire, or when we think (and sometimes say) "I don't know what to say."

Yet we have all seen at some point in time those who do know what to say, who animate the wavering, who comfort the bereaved, who inspire the hopeless, who convert people, who make people better, and who teach them.

While you have heard the expression "Sticks and stones can break my bones, but words can never hurt me!" We should know better than that! Words do matter.

Words penned by Leo Rosten in 1972 about the power of words, in my mind, speak loudly on the power of words. Ponder his expressions.

"Words—they sing, they hurt, they teach. They sanctify. They were man's first immeasurable feat of magic. They liberated us from ignorance and our barbarous past. For without these marvelous scribbles which build letters into words, words into sentences, sentences into systems and sciences and creeds, man would forever be confined to the self-isolated prison of the scuttle fish or the chimpanzee."

"One picture is worth ten thousand words" goes the timeworn Chinese maxim. But one writer tartly said, "It takes words to say that." We live by words—love, truth, God. We fight for words—freedom, country, and fame. We die for words—liberty, glory, and honor. They bestow the priceless gift of articulacy on our minds and hearts—from *"mama* to *infinity."* And the men who truly shape our destiny—the giants who teach us, inspire us, and lead us to deeds of immortality—are those who use words with clarity and passion.

In the fast-paced world that we live in, I sometimes wonder if we have gotten caught up in the world of the Internet, iPads, the Blackberry, Facebook, text messaging, and the ever-present e-mail mode, that we are slipping away from the wise, careful, and artful use of those little scribbles called WORDS.

Sometimes we are in such a hurry to "express ourselves" that we fail to truly pay attention to how we use words. I trust (yea, even pray) that we will not fall victim to the careless use of words.

I try to be careful, thoughtful, and artful in my choice and use of words. What about you?

ACKNOWLEDGMENTS AND DEDICATION

First and foremost, I must acknowledge the support and encouragement that I received from my late wife of fifty-five years—Bessie Ryan Lassiter. Without her steadfast support, comfort during times of stress and challenge, and encouragement, I would not have been able to have had a successful career. She had the capacity to think as I did, but to also provide needed perspectives. My heartfelt thanks to the "lady in black" who was the love of my life, and who continues to reside with me in spirit.

As will be noted in this book, my late father, Dr. Wright L. Lassiter Sr., was my first mentor and a lifelong coach and guide. Two other individuals played key mentorship roles. They were the distinguished president of Tuskegee University, the late Dr. Luther Hilton Foster, and the chancellor who brought me into the State University of New York System—Dr. Clifton R. Wharton Jr.

I also acknowledge and dedicate this book to a longtime colleague and friend—Dr. Curtis Ivery, chancellor of the Wayne County Community College District in Detroit, Michigan.

Finally, I want to acknowledge the many colleagues that I was privileged to work with at the various stages in my professional journey.

PART ONE

THE LIFE STORY IN ABSTRACT

I Shall Use My time
—Jack London

"I would rather be ashes than dust,
I would rather my spark should burn out in a brilliant blaze—
Than it should be stifled in dry-rot . . .
Man's chief purpose is to LIVE, not exist.
I shall not waste my days trying to prolong them.
I shall USE MY TIME."

A Gift of the River—Chancellor Emeritus
Plan Your Legacy Early
Career Interview
The Alcorn Experience
DCCCD First African-American Chancellor
The Role of the Chancellor
The "Largest Room" Context
Focus on Cultural Difference Interview
A Commitment to a Life of Service
The Role of Service
Let Your Life Speak
Nothing Much Happens Without a Dream
Dare to Follow Your Dreams

A GIFT OF THE RIVER

D r. Wright L. Lassiter Jr. is symbolic of that sacred Stone Age which had its beginning during the third millennium, finding an origin at Memphis—the capital of the Lower Region. He is a mental giant who towers above many who would claim to be his peers.

The native of Vicksburg, Mississippi, is the oldest of nine children, and he was the first member of the family to attend and graduate from college. Caring teachers nurtured him in his hometown of Vicksburg (on the Mississippi riverbanks), and later at Alcorn State University. As a result of those nurturing experiences, he confidently claims that "I am what family, teachers, and education enabled me to become."

The higher education and civic communities greeted Schenectady County Community College's presidential appointment in 1979 with open-mouthed surprise, and for apparent good reason. The youngest of the sixty-four institutions of the State University of New York System had tapped as its new leader a black man, Wright L. Lassiter Jr.—something the SUNY system had never done before, and something no one could have predicted. With that appointment, the SUNY system had its first ever black president.

In response to a reporter's question, his remarks were instructive. "The fact that I am black is, for me, just a part of my being—it is not something that I remark about. It is what I am . . . an accident of history that I rose from humble beginnings to have served as the president of three colleges and as the chancellor of the largest community college system in Texas (the Dallas County Community College District). And just by accident, that I became once again a "first." The first African American chancellor for that system. An accident, no more than that. But it also is recognition of the fact that I was fully prepared for each of those assignments."

The landscape is dotted with his achievements. He is the holder of two presidential appointments; twelve appointments by governors; service on numerous national boards and commissions, including many at the state and local levels; the recipient of an honorary degree (along with his four earned doctoral degrees; elected as a trustee of two universities; and countless citations and other accolades.

He is a veteran military officer, having served in the US Army during the reconstruction of the Republic of Korea following the Korean Conflict. He became one of the first non-physicians to serve as a hospital commander in the Army Reserve Medical Corps.

He is an ordained Baptist minister, the highest calling of man. In the words of Dr. Martin Luther King Jr., "He has charted a course toward greatness." King also said, "Every man can be great because every man can serve." Being touched by the fruits of education, he has touched others on his odyssey as an educator, administrator, and servant.

He is a published author, having written eleven books and collections of speeches and presentations in the form of monographs.

A strong family man, he and his late wife of fifty-five years (Bessie) have a daughter, a son, and two granddaughters.

Herodotus said of Egypt and its pyramids, "Egypt is a gift of the river—the mighty Nile."

Dr. Wright L. Lassiter Jr. is a great man—a gift of the mighty Mississippi River.

PLAN YOUR LEGACY EARLY

Upon graduation from Alcorn State University, I was invited to join the faculty for the summer session in 1955. Not only did I serve as the primary instructor in the Business Department of the college, but I also served as the acting department head for the summer. What an unexpected beginning for my career in higher education. Newly graduated with no teaching experience, but deemed fully capable of serving effectively in the classroom.

Following that short-term teaching appointment and experience, I was selected as a participant in a newly formed twelve-month Internship Training Program for College Business Officers at Tuskegee Institute. This was a bold step taken by the American Association of College Business Officers (the professional association for business officers in the historically black college and university sector of higher education) to plan for the entry of new prospects into that sphere of service.

Following completion of the program, I had a brief appointment as the investments accountant at Hampton Institute, which was cut short when I was drafted for service in the US Army, which included a tour in the Republic of Korea. I returned to Tuskegee Institute to resume my journey toward becoming the chief business officer of a college or university.

After serving in a variety of business officer positions at Tuskegee Institute (which included earning two graduate degrees), in 1976 I was privileged to move to the senior ranks in higher education administration when I was appointed the vice president for finance and management at Morgan State University in Baltimore, Maryland. With that decision made, I began planning for my departure from Tuskegee Institute where my career had been shaped and developed.

Prior to my departure, I had a final face-to-face period of reflection with a longtime friend and neighbor: Dr. Eugene W. Adams, a professor of veterinary medicine at the university. I recall that I shared with him that for just over seventeen years, my "professional bride" had been Tuskegee Institute. To such an extent that I had turned down numerous offers to leave the institution for advancement positions at other institutions. I had a dream of one day of becoming the CFO at that institution.

I had enjoyed a beautiful marriage; however, I said to my friend that from this point forward in my professional life, I would take on a "new bride." That new bride would be my career. As we exchanged thoughts, I even projected that prior to my retirement, I believed that I would make up to five professional moves. What thought! I further mused that from that point forward, I would also focus on the legacy that I wanted to leave as a leader in higher education administration. I had enjoyed an unbelievable developmental period at Tuskegee and had been shaped and molded by excellent mentors. Now I would need to take everything to a higher level, to include aiding others in their professional quests.

Thirty-eight years since leaving Tuskegee Institute to realize what was then my goal of rising to the level of chief financial officer of a medium-sized college or university, I have served as president of three colleges and as the chancellor of the seven-college Dallas County Community College District—the Dallas system being the largest community college system in Texas, enrolling over 105,000 full- and part-time students.

When I reflect on my journey, I feel compelled to share some key points with others about the legacy that I have endeavored to shape. It is not a normal pattern that one can serve as the president of not just one college, but three colleges. It is also not a normal pattern that the last college presidency spanned two decades, before I was asked to serve as the chancellor of the seven-college system in Dallas. It should be stated that I did not apply for the chancellorship; I was selected by the board of trustees, first as the interim chancellor. Twenty-three days later, they removed the "interim" designation after they had observed my early actions as chancellor.

I had occasion to thumb through an issue of the *Harvard Business Review* and saw an article that mirrored my thinking regarding legacy planning. Here are some pointers from that article that I have modified to fit my thinking.

- Your legacy is revealed in how your colleagues, employees, and others think and behave as a result of the time that they spent working with you.
- Do not make the mistake of thinking about your legacy as you near the end of your tenure or your career.
- Develop legacy thinking early in your career and make legacy thinking a catalyst for action in your career and life.
- Legacy thinking does a great thing for you as a leader.
- Legacy thinking reveals where your influence is having a lasting effect and where it does not.
- Thinking about leadership in the context of your legacy helps you establish priorities.
- Legacy thinking locates you in the history of the organization.
- Legacy thinking helps you recognize when you are wasting your time in a senior leadership position (or when your potential there has reached a plateau), and it is time for you to move on.
- Legacy thinking tempers your necessary focus on the tasks at hand with a sense of greater purpose.

Keep in mind that legacy thinking is like a two-edged sword. For younger leaders, legacies often change over time as you mature and become more self-aware. For more senior leaders, legacy thinking can expose regrets over roads not taken. At either extreme, legacy thinking can be unsettling or unfulfilling. But for all people in between, and even for those at either extreme, the potential upside from legacy thinking is greater.

Visioning and dreaming is a critical element in the planning pattern of a leader. On the wall of a church in England, there is a sign that reads: "A vision without a task is just a dream. A task without vision is drudgery. A vision and a task are the hope of the world."

Your work as a leader should always show that due consideration has been directed toward vision, task, hope, and the future.

In planning and living out your legacy, I commend an item written by Robert J. Hastings titled "The Station." Reflect on this selection by Hastings. These are just four lines from it; readers of this book who want the full document may contact me.

The Station

"In life, the journey is the joy. The station is an illusion—it constantly outdistances us. Yesterday is a memory, and tomorrow is a dream. Yesterday belongs to history; tomorrow belongs to God. Yesterday is a fading sunset, and tomorrow is a faint sunrise. Only in today is there light enough to love and live."

To both current and future leaders—begin planning your legacy now, wherever you are in life.

CAREER INTERVIEW

As the date for my retirement drew near, several requests for interviews came from local media reporters. What follows is the content of one such interview. It will be followed by a second interview where the focus was on my experiences at Alcorn College.

Career highlights and education. My entire professional career of five decades has been in the field of higher education. It began with my employment as a summer instructor at Alcorn State College immediately following my undergraduate graduation. Can you imagine being asked to join the faculty of a college with no teaching experience or an advanced degree? I was told that I distinguished myself beyond expectations as a student. I resided in the bachelor residence for male faculty members, and many of my former instructors gave me guidance as I needed it. After a year of advanced study in college business management at Tuskegee University, I was employed as an accountant at Hampton University, which was a brief period of employment as I was drafted for military duty that included service in the Republic of Korea during the reconstruction period following the Korean Conflict.

After military service, I returned to Tuskegee University, took on a wife, and joined the accounting staff. That was the next step as I began the journey seeking to become a college or university chief financial officer. Three years after returning to Tuskegee, I entered Indiana University where I earned an MBA degree. My career resumed following graduate school at Tuskegee University, and I advanced through promotions to the post of business manager of auxiliary enterprises. I also earned a doctorate in higher education and finance from Auburn University. One year following that achievement, I was appointed vice president for finance and management at Morgan State University (Baltimore, Maryland). With that appointment, I had realized my career goal of becoming the CFO of a university.

9

After four and a half years in that role, I was appointed president of Schenectady County Community College (New York) and served there for three and a half years. I subsequently served as the president of Bishop College in Dallas for three years and as president of El Centro College in the Dallas County Community College District. After twenty years as El Centro's president, I was named the sixth chancellor of the Dallas County Community College in 2006. I will retire as chancellor at the end of February and assume the title of chancellor emeritus—a distinction deemed appropriate by the board of trustees.

What I like best about my job. The opportunity to impact the lives of students and foster the development and growth of employees. In addition to making a difference with those stakeholders, I, along with my colleagues, serve as a vital cog in the "economic and community service engines" for Dallas County. Working with seven college presidents and vice chancellors, we play a major role in ensuring that the vision and mission of the district is realized and advanced. Working with my colleagues provides me with the privilege of displaying my commitment to being a servant leader.

The best advice that I have received for my current job. One of the trustees said to me, "You enter this role as chancellor with a vast amount of earned capital. Use it well." Advice from a previous mentor has served me well throughout my career. "Serving as a college president is a calling, not a job. Treat it that way and you will be successful."

What advice you would give a successor to your position as chancellor. Adherence to our vision and mission is a fundamental requirement for success here. Additionally, you must embrace the imperative of being collaborative and a team player and leader. Following my lead in being a servant leader would also be suggested. My mantra to everyone is "The largest room in any house is the room for improvement." Keep that thought clearly in focus.

If *you ever left work early, you could probably be found doing what.* I would first spend time with my wife. Then I would be either in my home office or library reading, writing commentaries for my weekly news organ, thinking about a sermon assignment, or putting the finishing touches on a book project. I have written eleven books.

People would be surprised to know that. I am an ordained Baptist minister and have served in various ministerial roles, including that of the interim pastor of an historic church in Dallas for three years (while serving as the president of El Centro College). They might also be surprised to know that I had served in the military, far beyond the initial service as a draftee. I retired from the US Army Reserves with the rank of lieutenant colonel. In my military service, I rose to the position of hospital commander and was one of the few hospital commanders who was not a physician. I also taught in the Army Command and General Staff College. Very few people know that I have received two presidential appointments for national service.

One thing you wish more people knew about the Dallas District. Employees work in the Dallas District because they want to be part of an organization that is committed to "changing lives." They choose to serve because of the opportunity to make a difference in the lives of students, and also to enhance economic development in the Greater Dallas area.

This is a brief exposure into my life as I prepare to move to postretirement.

THE ALCORN EXPERIENCE

D*escribe your experiences at Alcorn.* I am the oldest of nine children and was the first to attend and graduate from college. I was initially disappointed upon my enrollment as the major in business administration (my choice) was discontinued and replaced with a major in business education. I reluctantly agreed to attend and major in business education, which was preparation for public school teaching. I wanted to withdraw after one week. However, the assistant dean of men convinced my parents to let me stay, and he would work with me to adjust to college. That was a wise decision.

A pleasant experience was that I was given advanced credit for the typing and business communication courses based on my high school performance. As a result of those "plus" experiences, my counselor suggested that I enroll in a junior-level psychology course. I entered the class and immediately encountered upper-class students and elected to drop the course. The course was taught by Professor Hance Gamblin. Later in my time at Alcorn, he and I became conversational friends, and he chided me for dropping the course, which was an important lesson on being a risk-taker.

I was a work-study student for all four years, beginning as the student secretary in the superintendent of buildings and grounds office (a former high school teacher in my hometown of Vicksburg, Mississippi) and ending as the student secretary in the office of the president. In my junior year, I was selected as a student member of the college counseling corps. My student teaching was in Greenwood, Mississippi. It was a good experience; however, I came away not at all inspired over the prospects of a career as a public school teacher. I graduated magna cum laude and the number 2 ranking in the graduating class.

In what ways did Alcorn contribute to your career path? Two things are noteworthy. In the second semester of my senior year, I was working as a student secretary in the president's office. One afternoon, the college business manager, Mr. J. A. Ramos, visited with me and told me about a new training program that had been established to prepare young African American men for a career as college business managers. The program was first of its kind and had been established by the American Association of College Business Officers, to prepare for a career in college business management. The training was conducted at Tuskegee Institute. He strongly encouraged me to apply for the program, and I accepted his advice. I was invited for an interview—an early success. The president of Alcorn was Dr. J. R. Otis, who had come to Alcorn from Tuskegee (he had been dean of the school of agriculture there), and he still maintained his home in Tuskegee. When I told him about the development, he invited me to ride with him to Tuskegee. I received presidential lectures going and returning. I was accepted for the program, and I attribute my collegiate experiences as a factor. The twelve-month training experience was to begin in September 1955.

A second event at Alcorn was most significant. On the day of graduation, just prior to leaving with my parents for home in Vicksburg, the head of the business department, Mr. Jimmie King, approached me and asked if I had a job for the summer—or better still, he said, would I be willing to stay at Alcorn and join the faculty for the summer? My response was "If you have enough confidence in me to believe that I can be a credible college teacher, I am enough of a risk-taker to say yes." That was the beginning of my higher education journey.

On the next day, I reported to Mr. King to receive my teaching assignment. I knew nothing about teaching loads, so I agreed to teach three classes (accounting principles, business communication, and shorthand). After receiving the textbooks and other materials, I prepared to leave his office when he said, "There has been another development, Wright. I have to be away for the summer as my mother is quite ill. You will have to be the acting department head as well as the instructor for the three summer classes." What a transition from walking across the stage at commencement on Sunday and, on Monday, being a faculty member and a department head.

The next day, I entered my classroom to teach my first class in accounting principles. After placing all my materials on my desk, I looked up and who was sitting in front of me was my favorite high school teacher—Mrs. Rosa Parrott. Here I am, a rookie teacher facing someone that I viewed as an outstanding teacher. The challenge of being a risk taker, having courage, and being prepared were early lessons from the Alcorn experience. At the conclusion of the class, Mrs. Parrot said to me, "You were the best college instructor that I have had thus far at Alcorn!" I could not have asked for more encouragement.

Upon completing the training program at Tuskegee, my first position in the business field was at Hampton Institute (now Hampton University) as the investments accountant. Alcorn prepared me for that, along with Tuskegee Institute. My work at Hampton was interrupted when I was drafted in the US Army and served in the post–Korean Conflict period. Upon the conclusion of military service, I resumed my career at Tuskegee Institute.

After serving in accounting positions for three years, I entered the MBA program at Indiana University. When I registered, the MBA management program director, Dr. John Mee, reviewed my Alcorn transcript and gave me advanced credit for three of my graduate classes! If I had trepidations about the value of my experience at Alcorn, they were all dashed with that positive action. The Alcorn experience prepared me for my first graduate study program.

After seventeen years at Tuskegee and the earning of my doctorate, I accepted the chief business officer position at Morgan State University. Alcorn prepared me for a successful career at Tuskegee and, subsequently, at Morgan State University.

A favorite memory of my Alcorn days was the nurturing culture that I experienced and participated in. I have carried those experiences with me at all of my career points.

I never dreamed of serving as the president of a college or university while at Alcorn. My ultimate career objective was to serve as the chief financial officer of a college or university. When I reached that goal by being invited to join the administration at Morgan State University, I considered that I had reached the pinnacle on my career journey.

Two years into my service at Morgan, a friend and neighbor approached me and suggested that I agree to have my name placed in nomination for the presidency of Virginia Union University. I had never envisioned being a college president, nor was that a career goal. I called my mentor (the president of Tuskegee Institute), who gave me sage advice regarding the presidency and preparation for it. After our visit, I concluded that I was not ready for that challenge. Two and a half years later, I did apply for the presidency of Schenectady County Community College (in the State University of New York System) and was selected. It is still somewhat unusual for an individual to be selected as a president on his/her initial effort as I had been. Upon my election to that post, I became the first African American president in the State University of New York System in 1980. Ironically, I was named president by the first African American chancellor for the system—Dr. Clifton R. Wharton, an internationally recognized leader.

My career then progressed when I served as the president of Bishop College for three years, president of El Centro College of the Dallas County Community College District for twenty years, and now serving as chancellor of the Dallas System since 2006. The Dallas District is the largest community college system in Texas with seven separately accredited colleges and a total enrollment of more than 105,000 students. How my scope has enlarged since leaving Alcorn.

Long before I read and studied the concepts of servant leadership, as I reflect on my Alcorn experiences, I was exposed to servant leadership there. In addition to servant leadership, I have been a mentor, coach, and guide to many of my colleagues and associates. The seeds for that were planted at Alcorn, and these blossomed later in life.

While at Tuskegee, I was exposed to the early life of Dr. Martin Luther King Jr., the Montgomery Bus Boycott, and the entire cycle of events associated with the civil rights era.

As a young adult, my father shared a thought with me that has been a part of me and my leadership.

Another aspect of my leadership pattern is "the largest room in any house is the room for improvement" pattern. He said, "Junior, service is the rent that you pay for the space that you occupy on earth." Later, he added a little postscript when he said, "Always strive to live in a high-rent district."

DCCCD FIRST AFRICAN AMERICAN CHANCELLOR

During a special meeting of the Dallas County Community College District's board of trustees on June 12, 2006, members unanimously appointed Dr. Wright L. Lassiter Jr. as its sixth and first African American chancellor. Lassiter recently assumed the duties of interim chancellor following the resignation of Dr. Jesus "Jess" Carreon in May.

It is not uncommon for a board of trustees to take up to twelve months to go through a search process and select a new president or chancellor. It only took the Dallas District trustees thirty days to determine that the longtime president of El Centro College was the person "already on board" to lead the seven colleges of the Dallas County Community College with a current enrollment that exceeds 64,000 credit students.

"We are pleased to appoint Dr. Wright Lassiter chancellor of the Dallas County Community College District. We congratulate Dr. Lassiter, and we are very proud of him," said Jerry Prater, chair of the district's board of trustees. "He has wrapped his arms around the task of leading the Dallas District in such a remarkable way that we concluded that a lengthy search process was not necessary. We had our man already here."

"I will live up to your confidence in me," said Lassiter to the DCCCD trustees. "Serving as chancellor will be challenging, and I welcome the task as I am confident that I will have the collaboration and support of my colleagues at each of the district's seven colleges—Brookhaven, Cedar Valley, Eastfield, El Centro, Mountain View, North Lake, and Richland—as we move forward with the business of educating our students," said Lassiter.

Lassiter joined the Dallas District as president of El Centro College in 1986. Prior to that time, he served as president of Bishop College (Dallas); president of Schenectady County Community College (New York); vice president for finance and administration at Morgan State University (Baltimore, Maryland); and director of auxiliary enterprises/ business manager at Tuskegee University (then Tuskegee Institute in Tuskegee, Alabama). He served as a faculty member at Tuskegee and Morgan State in addition to his administrative duties.

He holds a bachelor's degree in business from Alcorn State University (Mississippi), a master's degree in business administration from Indiana University, and his doctorate in educational administration and finance from Auburn University (Alabama).

He is a native of Vicksburg, Mississippi. He is married and has two adult children and two granddaughters.

Ann Hatch—District Office of Marketing and Communications

THE ROLE OF THE CHANCELLOR

I am frequently asked—"what is the job of the chancellor?" In responding to that question, I inform the questioner of the uniqueness of the DCCCD. That is, we are a multicollege district (conversely not a multicampus district) consisting of seven separately accredited colleges, with a president (chief executive officer) for each college. The presidents are accountable to the chancellor, who in turn is accountable to the board of trustees.

The presidents have the responsibility for the operations of the colleges. The chancellor provides overall direction in furtherance of the mission of the district. The chancellor is the "public voice and face" functioning as the internal and external representative of the district. Accordingly, that role is also discharged by the presidents in their respective service areas. It could be said that the chancellor is the number 1 salesperson and advocate in behalf of the overall district.

The chancellor and the college chief executive officers should engage in the discharge of their duties from seven leadership perspectives that are essential for success. Each should be:

➢ VISIONARY. A visionary is committed to growth, looks beyond immediate problems to identify root causes, and develops precise steps of action to achieve success.
➢ TEACHER. A teacher imparts wisdom, maturity, and skill to others; validates direction; and ensures completeness.
➢ SERVER. A server sees and meets practical needs of others, freeing them to accomplish their goals, and invests time and energy to their success.

➤ ORGANIZER. An organizer visualizes final results and directs resources for the successful completion of goals.

➤ MEDIATOR. A mediator is deeply loyal, compassionate, and analyzes the benefits and problems of a given direction.

➤ IDEALIST. An idealist must have unimpeachable integrity, be open to correction, be willing to identify problems as they arise, and speak the truth boldly.

➤ PROVIDER. A provider is resourceful, prudent, thrifty, and constantly ensuring the best use of all available resources.

➤ EQUIPPER. Equipping is a tough job, but it must be artfully and strategically engaged in. In my view, if a leader wishes to equip those that they lead, they must give them certain gifts:

- I must CARE for them (Communication, Affirmation, Recognition, and Example).
- I must work on their weaknesses, but work out their strengths.
- I must give them myself (time, energy, and focus).
- I must give them ownership of their respective roles.
- I must become a resource person myself (atmosphere, training, support, and tools).
- I must make expectations clear.
- I must eliminate unnecessary burdens.
- I must catch them doing something good, and then reward them.

Think of the chancellor and the president as a coach, building the team. How do they build a diverse group into a unified and collaborative team? These questions are instructive:

- Am I building people, or building my "kingdom" and using people?
- Do I care enough to confront people when it will make a difference?
- Am I listening with more than my ears?
- Am I asking the right questions to develop the right relationships?
- What are the major strengths of each member of the team?
- Have I placed a high priority on their jobs?
- Have I shown the value they will receive from their work?
- Are their goals compatible with mine?

Executive Coach Marshall Goldsmith, author of *What Got You Here Won't Get You There*, says every leader's Job One is getting the best from his or her people. His advice is directed toward how to manage your team during a period of crisis.

- JUDGE LESS. Realize that any unusual behavior may have deeper causes. Be more empathetic and tolerant than usual.
- HELP THOSE WHO ARE DOWN. Some employees are dealing with unusual amounts of stress. Help them now, and they will be loyal later.
- FOCUS ON THE FUTURE. Everyone wants to talk about "what could have been." Forget it. Get your team focused on what lies ahead.
- UNDERSTAND YOUR EMOTIONS. You may be feeling stressed, angry, and insecure. Get help. Be professional, and don't take it out on your team.

I read where someone said "What does the chancellor do besides write the Weekend Memo and occasional bulletins?" I trust that I have provided insight into the work required to serve as the chief executive officer of the largest community college system in Texas, as well as the largest undergraduate institution in the state. I wonder if there are any takers for this job when I retire.

THE "LARGEST ROOM"
CONTEXT

The largest room in our house is the room for improvement.

In my previous life as a college president, I would often pose this question to my colleagues: "What is the largest room in any house?" After concluding that it was a trick question, I would provide the answer: "The largest room in any house is the room for improvement." I ask all my colleagues and associates to impress that powerful thought in their work and in their lives.

The remarks of the new president of Harvard University at that time—Dr. Drew Gilpin Faust—are instructive as relates to collaboration. The purpose of this piece is to share a few nuggets from her talk, and to offer suggestions on how to capitalize on the experiences of each team member, and a few thoughts on attitudes.

Dr. Faust was an unlikely choice as the president of Harvard. As I read her remarks regarding her appointment, they seemed to parallel my appointment as chancellor.

- "Our shared enterprise is to make Harvard's future even more remarkable than the past."
- "This will mean recognizing and building on what we already do well. It will also mean recognizing what we don't do as well as we should—and being content until we find ways to do better."
- "We face extraordinary opportunities. But if we at Harvard are to accomplish all we intend, we need to find new ways of working together, of engaging the creativity of one of the most talented communities in the world."

·   "We need to break down barriers that inhibit collaboration among schools or disciplines, barriers that divide the sciences and the humanities into what C. P. Snow once famously called two cultures, barriers that separate the practice of the arts from the interpretations of the arts, barriers that lead us to identify ourselves as from one or the other 'side of the river.' Collaboration means more energy, more ideas, more wisdom; it also means investing beyond one's own particular interest or bailiwick. It means learning to live and to think within the context of the whole university."

We could easily replace the words *Harvard* and *University* with the Dallas County Community College District and your location, and those phrases would resonate with the words that you have heard from me on the subject of collaboration and trust.

In their book, *The Accidental Leader*, Harvey Robbins and Michael Finley outlined several things that we need to learn and practice in order to take advantage of the set of unique talents, gifts, and lessons resident in each of us. Consider these three suggestions from their book as they relate to collaboration and teamwork.

·   Learn how long each team member has been with the organization.
·   Learn who has had experiences with teamwork. Find out who has been part of an effective collaborative team. It may tell you how to organize future tasks and assignments.
·   Learn the most fulfilling work experiences each team member has ever had. Their answers will tell you what you need to do to create a more positive and collaborative work environment.

Those suggestions move beyond experiences to inform one that individuals on teams and in organizations come with a set of expectations. Do you know what they are, or are you merely guessing? It is an uphill battle if you do not address the subject of expectations.

·   Learn what your team members want. What motivates them?
·   Learn their mission expectations. Do they understand the team's mission? Do they have any doubts or reservations? You cannot presume they automatically "get it" and are on board.
·   Learn your team's expectations of a leader.

Now to the third point in this commentary—attitude. I recall reading where a young PhD was about to get his first teaching assignment. He had simply "wowed" the search committee, and they had nothing but good comments to make about him. He sat for the final session with the crusty dean. The dean's remarks really caught his attention. The dean said, "It looks like you're a good kid—darn good. But I'll tell you this. I run a positive team around here, and that comes first. I don't care how good of a teacher you are. If I hire you . . . and you ruin that team, you're out of here. You got that?"

The young PhD was hired because he entered the situation with an early lesson. Being good at something is never good enough. You've got to have more than expertise. You've got to have the right attitude and people skills to fit in, excel, and succeed.

Charles Swindoll says the same thing with this expression: "Your attitude will determine your altitude."

Zig Ziglar says the same thing in his book *Over the Top*. "Skill alone will not take you over the top—or keep you there. You might possess the most advanced skill set in your profession, but if you have a doom-and-gloom attitude, you will become a liability to yourself, your team, and your organization. Peak performance can only be attained with the powerful combination of excellent skill and positive, proactive attitude."

I have seen too many instances when attitude is not given enough consideration. Fortunately, there is a growing number of adherents to the criticality of attitude. Consider the great football coach Lou Holz who says, "Ability is what you are capable of doing. Motivation determines what you do. Attitude determines how well you do it."

In fact, your attitude will imprison you or embolden you. Now consider the late African American who founded *Ebony* and *Jet* magazines, John Johnson. Starting out at the bottom, with nothing, dealing with discrimination and unfair treatment, he pulled himself to the top of the business world with his attitude. Johnson says, "Men and women are limited not by the place of their birth, not by the color of their skin, but the size of their hope." Johnson is absolutely correct, and his life is a testimony to the importance of having a positive attitude. He took out a loan of $500 on his mother's furniture, and as the late Paul Harvey would say, "You know the rest of that story."

But some people don't know what it means to have a positive attitude. They always operate from the mentality of the "glass is half empty," rather than the "glass is half full." Some people think if they have a positive attitude, they will always be happy. Or they will never have a problem. Wrong! It is not possible to be happy all the time. And life will always give you plenty of problems. But a positive attitude will give you the energy to get through your problems and feel better more quickly.

William Arthur Ward gives one of the best definitions of a positive attitude. Ward says, "Real optimism is aware of problems, but recognizes solutions; knows about difficulties, but believes they can be overcome; sees the negatives, but accentuates the positive; is exposed to the worst, but expects the best; and has reason to complain, but chooses to smile."

When you look at Ward's definition, how do you stack up? No matter what your role is, no matter where you are now, your attitude is one of the most powerful forces you have working for you (or against you). And there is no better time than now to build your attitude. Using Ward's definition, answer these questions about yourself. If you do not like your answers, decide to go to work on your attitude.

- Are you more aware of the possible solutions in your life and work? Are you focused more upon the problems?
- Do you believe your difficulties can be overcome?
- Do you believe you are simply stuck with those difficulties?
- Do you see the negatives, but accentuate the positives?
- Can you see the best even when you're exposed to the worst?

If you find yourself focusing more on the negative aspects of your life than the positive, it may be time for an attitude adjustment. I would suggest that you read Dr. Alan Zimmerman's book titled *Pivot*. It could be a life and attitude changer for you.

Your attitude determines your altitude. In other words, if you want to go higher or achieve more, if you want your college or your location to move toward becoming a great entity, you've got to have the right attitude. And there is good news: anyone can have the right attitude. Also, do not forget that *being good at something is never good enough.* Just food for thought.

FOCUS ON CULTURAL DIFFERENCES INTERVIEW

Describe any early experiences. In the summer of 1954, while working with my father on a contracting job at the Spencer Chemical Works in Vicksburg, I was asked to report to the payroll office because a staff member who had been habitually absent on payroll preparation day was again absent. The superintendent had heard my father speaking about my typing and mathematical abilities. I walked into that all-white office and completed the assignment in just a few hours. When I gave the finished work to the superintendent, he informed that there was nothing else to do and I could return to work with my father.

The next day, the employee that I had replaced for a few hours and her husband resigned from the company because a black person had sat in her chair and at her desk. The office staff made fun of her because a black man had finished her work so quickly. This is one of those "firsts" that never make the headlines, but they provide valuable learning experiences on how to embrace cultural differences. Things were very different in 1954.

Following college and my first graduate degree experience, I was appointed to the Tuskegee (Alabama) Housing Authority and was elected chairman of the board in 1964. My first task was to integrate the formerly all-white housing operations and its all-white staff in 1965. This was a result of implementing the Civil Rights Act of 1965 signed into law by President Lyndon Johnson. A few months earlier, I was returning from a brief vacation in Baltimore with my wife and our two young children. We were traveling by car. During those days, there were essentially no hotel or motel accommodations for persons of color. Therefore, in most cases, you just kept driving. Or if you had to stop, you parked your car at a service station, under a light, and slept in your car. We had reached Rome, Georgia, and I was totally exhausted and could not drive safely any longer. I told my wife that the Civil Rights Act had been passed, and this was a good time to test it. She was frightened and begged me to not make any trouble and maybe leave her as a widow.

I persisted and walked into the front door of the Downtown Hotel Rome. I said to the clerk, "I would like a room for me and my family." To my pleasant surprise, he handed me the registration materials. I received the key to our room and went back to my bewildered wife to tell her what had happened. I parked our car in the "regular" parking lot, and we went to our room.

The next morning, my wife now had courage on her own, and she called down for an iron to press the clothes for our children. Within minutes, a worker appears with an iron and ironing board and politely asks, "Will there be anything else?"

We packed and went down to the restaurant for breakfast—through the front door. After our orders had been taken, I glanced toward the rear of the room and saw all of the Negro kitchen staff just staring at us and smiling. We were the first persons to integrate that establishment.

This additional comment about the Tuskegee Housing Authority may be noteworthy. At the conclusion of my eight-year term as chairman of the board of directors, the Tuskegee Housing Authority was nationally recognized for integration and community relations. In addition, we became one of the first agencies to introduce a home ownership plan for residents. Can you envision the challenges that a leader faced in realizing those results in the Deep South that had not shed its segregationist beliefs and practices?

My undergraduate and graduate experiences and the first twenty-one years of my professional life were spent in the historically black college setting with a mind-set of embracing cultural competence. The first seventeen years were spent at Tuskegee Institute, founded by Booker T. Washington. I carefully studied the practices of that legendary founder of the university and national education leader.

Where and how long have you lived in different cultures? Living in the segregated South was a unique cultural experience. I lived in the Republic of Korea for a period of seventeen months during military service. My travels have been to the following places: United Kingdom, South Africa,

Brazil, Taiwan, the Republic of China, Japan, Mexico, Canada, and South American cities on cruises and vacations.

What kinds of family experiences have you had around cultural differences? My wife and I began hosting interracial gatherings at our home in Tuskegee, and every other city where we have lived.

I served on the International Visitors Committee of the Dallas Commission on World Affairs. As a member, my wife and I hosted international visitors at our home and El Centro College. The visitors at our home were from China, Taiwan, Mexico, South Korea, Iraq, Russia, Germany, and other smaller European countries.

Have there been other specific initiatives? I was the founder of the Dallas Blueprint for Leadership at the United Way of Metropolitan Dallas. The program was designed to prepare ethnic minorities for effective service on boards and commissions that received funding from United Way. Cultural differences were a part of the curriculum.

I created the position of college ombudsman at El Centro College. That staff member, who reported to the college president, played a critical role in our efforts to encourage and embrace the concept of "cultural competence."

The Visiting Scholars Program was created with the objective of enhancing the presence of persons of color and other cultures as members of the faculty. About 95 percent of the participants completed the two-year program and transitioned into regular faculty positions.

Worldview: What is your philosophy or viewpoint around cultural differences broadly? I believe in the inherent worth of all persons and that we should appreciate cultural differences. Appreciation means understanding of differences rather than the acceptance of all differences.

How do you see the relationship of community and cultural differences among all people? My orientation as a Baptist minister and theologian, as well as a professor of ethics, has had a significant impact on my views. We should have a strong commitment to the concept of cultural competence.

An obvious obstacle is the resistance of many elements of the overall populace that fails to embrace the concept of cultural competence. Additionally, to come to appreciate the worth of all persons regardless of race, ethnicity, and economic and social standing.

Having been the "first" African American in a number of settings, I have faced every possible challenge that we could expect of a personal nature. As a result I do not face any so-called great challenge from a personal perspective. I try to live by the mantra "The largest room in any house is the room for improvement." The challenge is to continue pushing for cultural understanding.

The culture of an organization is viewed by the masses as the "way things are done" in that organization. Based on that truth, the core values of trust, respect, openness, transparency, and civility should guide and influence all aspects of an organization.

LET YOUR LIFE SPEAK

One of my favorite expressions is "Success is achieved through effort, determination, and perseverance." Can you relate to that expression? One of my favorite authors is Parker Palmer. In his book *Let Your Life Speak*, he offers these powerful thoughts regarding learning. I have chosen the title of his book for my address to this assembly on today. Reflect on these points:

- We learn by listening with care to our own inner voice.
- We learn from our gifts.
- We learn from what makes us happy.
- We learn from our mistakes.
- We learn from our limitations.
- We learn from our childhood memories.
- We learn from hardship and difficulty.
- We learn from excuses.
- We learn from our fears.

Today often falls to pieces—so what is the missing piece? Ask yourself this question: how often do you have a great day? Is today the norm or the rare exception for you? How would you rate today? So far today, has it been a great day? Has today been less wonderful thus far? Ask this question: how does today impact tomorrow's success? Everyone wants to have a good day, but not many people know what a good day looks like—much less how to create one. And even fewer people understand how the way you live today impacts your tomorrow. Why is that so? The root of the problem is that most people misunderstand success. If we have a faulty view of success, we have a faulty approach to our day. As a result, today falls to pieces.

Now I want to share with you, at this stage in your professional lives, some common misconceptions concerning success and the response that often go with them.

We believe success is impossible—so we criticize it. M. Scott Peck opened his best-selling book *The Road Less Traveled* with the words "Life is difficult." He went on to say, "Most do not fully see this truth that life is difficult. Instead, they moan more or less incessantly . . . about the enormity of their problems, their burdens, and their difficulties as if life was generally easy, so we sometimes assume anything that is difficult must be impossible."

We believe success is mystical—so we search for it. If success has escaped us, yet we have not entirely given up on it, then we often see it as a big mystery. We believe that all we need is the magic formula, the silver bullet, or the golden key that will solve all of our problems. You can relate to the fact that we have all of these magic diet programs and formulas, books, and assorted fads.

The problem is that we want the rewards of success without paying the price. You don't win the Olympic gold medal with a few weeks of intense training. There is no such thing as an overnight opera sensation. Great law firms or design companies do not spring up overnight. No chiropractic practice just magically emerges. There is no magic solution to success.

We believe success comes from luck—so we hope for it. You have heard it said that "he was just in the right place at the right time" to explain away someone else's success. That is a myth just like the idea of the overnight success.

We believe success is productivity—so we work for it. There was this sign posted in a small business window that said: "The 57 Rules of Success. #1 Deliver the goods. #2—The other 56 don't matter." There is something to be said for working hard and producing results that feel very rewarding to you. But seeing hard work as success is one-dimensional.

We believe success comes from an opportunity—so we wait for it. Many of the people who work very hard yet don't seem to get anywhere believe that the only thing they need is a break. Their motto begins with the words "If only."

The truth is that people who do nothing more than wait for an opportunity won't be ready to capitalize on one if it does appear. Basketball legend John Wooden said, "When opportunity comes, it is too late to prepare." An opportunity may help you, but it will not guarantee success.

We believe success comes from leverage—so we power up for it. Some people associate success with power. The industrialist Andrew Carnegie once asserted, "Success is the power with which to acquire whatever one demands of life, without violating the rights of others." Many people take their view of success and power one step further, assuming that successful people have taken advantage of others to get where they are. So to get what they want, they look for an angle to exploit or for leverage over someone else. You cannot force your way into success.

We believe success comes from connections—so we network for it. There are people who believe that if they just had the connections, they would have it made. That is faulty thinking.

We believe success comes from recognition—so we strive for it. In your profession, is there a sure sign that you have made it? Listen to this story. France is a nation of food lovers where chefs receive the highest honor. One of the highest marks of recognition is a three-star rating for a restaurant from the Michelin guide. There are only twenty-five such restaurants in all of France. One of them is an establishment in the Burgundy region owned by Bernard Loiseau called the Côte d'Or.

For decades, the chef was said to have been so obsessed with creating the perfect restaurant and receiving the highest award by Michelin. He worked harder and harder and, in 1981, received the two-star rating. He perfected each dish on his menu. He improved the service of the restaurant. He went $5 million in debt to improve and expand his facility. Finally, in 1991, he received his third star. He had accomplished what only a handful of others could achieve.

He once said, "We are selling dreams. We are merchants of happiness." But the recognition he received did not keep him happy. In the spring of 2003, after the lunch service, he committed suicide by shooting himself. He didn't warn anyone, nor did he leave a note. Some say he was disconnected because his rating in another restaurant guide had fallen from seventeen to nineteen (out of twenty). Others described him as a maniac depressive. No one will ever know why he killed himself, but we can be sure that the great recognition he had received in his profession was not enough for him.

As I said at the beginning of this talk, today matters. Many people miss that point. You may ask, what do you mean by that statement? The statement is true for these reasons: (1) We overexaggerate yesterday. It may sound trite, but today is the only time you have. It is too late for yesterday, and you cannot depend on tomorrow. (2) We overestimate tomorrow. (3) We underestimate today.

Make the Number 1 Decision—Then Manage It Daily

You will learn that there are only a handful of important decisions people need to make in their entire lifetimes. Does that surprise you? Most people complicate life and get bogged down in decision-making. Successful people make the right decisions early and manage those decisions daily. The earlier you make those right decisions and the longer you manage them, the more successful you can become. The people who neglect to make those decisions, and to manage them well, often look back on their lives with pain and regret—no matter how much talent they possessed or how many opportunities they once had.

Regret in the End

A classic example such a person was Oscar Wilde. A poet, playwright, novelist, and critic, Wilde was a man of unlimited potential. Born in 1854, he won scholarships and was educated in Britain's best schools. He excelled in Greek, winning the Gold Medal at Trinity College for his studies. He was awarded the Newdigate Prize and was honored as "First in Greats" at Oxford. His plays were popular and earned him lots of money, and he was the toast of London. His talent seemed limitless. Yet at the end of his life, he was broken and miserable. His wanton life landed him in prison. From jail, he wrote a perspective on his life. In it, he said these words:

"I was a man who stood in symbolic relations to the art and culture of my age. I had realized this for myself at the very dawn of my manhood, and had forced my age to realize it afterwards. Few men hold such a position in their own lifetime, and have it so acknowledged, it is usually discerned, if it is discerned at all, by the historian or the critic, long after both the man and his age have passed away. With me it was different. I felt it myself and made others feel it. Byron was a symbolic figure, but his relations were to the passion of his age and its weariness of passion. Mine were to something more viable, more permanent, of more vital issue, of larger scope.

The gods had given me almost everything. But I let myself be lured into long spells of senseless and sensual ease. I amused myself with being a dandy, a man of fashion. I surrounded myself with the smaller natures and the meaner minds. I became the spendthrift of my own genius, and to waste an eternal youth gave me a curious joy. Tired of being on the heights, I deliberately went to the depths in search for new sensation. What the paradox was to me in the sphere of thought, perversity became to me in the sphere of passion. Desire, at the end, was a malady or madness, or both. I grew careless of the lives of others. I took pleasure where it pleased me, and passed on. I forgot that every little action of the common day makes or unmakes character, and that therefore what one has done in the secret chamber, one has some day to cry aloud on the housetop. I ceased to be lord over myself. I allowed pleasure to dominate me. I ended in horrible disgrace."

By the time Wilde saw where his inattention to the day was going to land him, it was too late. He lost his family, his fortune, his self-respect, and even his will to live. He died bankrupt and broken at age forty-six.

Concluding Thoughts

I believe that everyone has the power to impact the outcome of his life. The way to do it is to focus initially on today. Benjamin Franklin rightly observed, "One today is worth two tomorrows. What I am to be, I am now becoming." You can make a good day—in fact, you can make today a masterpiece. Today is the only time we have within our grasp, yet many people let it slip through their fingers. They recognize neither today's value nor its potential. The earlier you make those right decisions and the longer you manage them, the more successful you can become.

I draw your attention to just four lines from a piece written by John Murphy entitled "Habits Die Hard." As stated in a previous item in this book, if you want the full text, just contact me. These are the lines, and they relate to habits.

"You can run me for profit, or you can run me for ruin. Show me how you want it done. Educate me. Train me. Lead me. Reward me.

And I will then do it automatically; I am your servant. Who am I? I am a habit."

All great leaders share a common belief, which they practice and also pass on to others. If you make good habits, good habits will make you. This wisdom has been around since ancient times. In fact, it was Aristotle who said, "Excellence is not an act—it's a habit."

Here's the point. Habits, be they good or bad, are difficult to break. Therefore the challenge for all persons in an organization is to determine the good habits that will be the drivers for success. Once the desired habits are identified, good training and continual reinforcement are critical in making them part of who you are. This is food for thought, and for you in this Parker College program, it starts with how you address today.

NOTHING MUCH HAPPENS
WITHOUT A DREAM

I am pleased to be addressing a cadre of new and eager scholars. What shall I talk with you about? First of all, let me inform you that this group represents the elite of the college. You have already demonstrated the capacity to achieve at a high level on a consistent basis, as evidenced by your grade point averages.

If I had the time, I could talk with you about change and how difficult it is for some people to deal with change. After all, we cannot depend on anything today—the decisions we make today may not work tomorrow. But it is important that we start thinking about change in a positive way and not dread change. But that subject would extend me beyond the time given me to talk.

If I had the time, I could talk about the massive world changes, but we do not have the time for that kind of discourse. If I had the time, we could talk about the critical need for educational reform in America. If I had the time, I could tell you that if this country does not take action now to reform our educational system, our nation may never regain our stature as a competitive and leading force in the world.

So what will I talk about? Let me share a thought which you can view as being "transportable." You can carry it with you as you prepare and plan for your futures. That thought is "Nothing much happens without a dream!"

I can recall that when I was in school, those persons who were "dreamers" were written off. It meant that you were not practical, you did not pay attention, and perhaps you were in another world, or "spaced out." But I want to pass on to you that it is through dreams that we accomplish things. One example is the universe of colleges and universities that populate our nation. The founders of those institutions had dreams.

The California Angels baseball team has a remarkable player named Jim Abbott. Abbott had a dream. It takes a special kind of person to make a dream come through against all odds. Jim was born without a right hand. His parents raised this remarkable man by treating him "remarkably." Abbott said in an interview, "I always pictured myself as a baseball pitcher, but I can't remember how many hands I had in my dreams. I just went out and did things." And he has certainly done things, for he was a big league pitcher—not a freak of nature. He also won games as a pitcher in his time with the Angels.

Greg Lemond had a dream. He dreamed he could be the first American to win the greatest bicycle race in the world—the grueling 2,000-mile Tour de France. And he did win. But it wasn't that easy. It came about because of an accident in 1986, when he was accidentally shot while hunting. He was near death with fifty shotgun pellets in his body. In that hospital bed, he had another dream. He dreamed that he would live, and that he would race again. He did both.

Dreams come all around us. Lee Iacocca had a dream. Walt Disney had a dream. Steve Jobs had a dream. John Johnson who founded *Ebony* magazine had a dream. I had a dream of being a college president. But for the next few minutes, I want to talk with you about your dreams.

Being inducted into this honor society has to be part of you living out a dream. However, this is only the beginning. Now, I want you to do something. Take the time, right now. Close your eyes and dream a wild, impossible, crazy dream for your future.

Visualize where you want to be—what you want to be doing—in five years, ten years, twenty years. Hold on to that single vision, and when you go home, write it down on a piece of paper and take good care of it. In the months and years to come, especially if you feel that you have lost your way, take out that piece of paper and dream all over again. Take the time do this, and the chances are your dream will be a dream no longer. It will be a reality, and only you—no one else—will have made it so. Think big dreams, students! Now a personal episode to conclude my time with you.

It was my privilege to join with a group of African American college presidents—Chuck Green, Homer Franklin, Roy Phillips, and Richard Turner, as we had a dream—the audacious idea that we could find a way to "prime the pump" and work to prepare African American men and women for leadership positions in higher education.

In my case, I remembered the counsel that I received from my mentor, the late Dr. Luther Hilton Foster Jr., when I was approached regarding having my name placed in nomination for the presidency of Virginia Union University. Among the sage words that I received from him were these: "The effective president is one who has the capacity to lead leaders." Taking that counsel to heart, I spent two and a half years engaged in a rigorous program of preparation, and then I applied for the presidency of Schenectady County Community College. To the surprise of many, I was successful in my first attempt—because I had a dream and worked hard to achieve it.

Each of the persons named earlier had climbed the ladder to become a college president, and we dreamed that others could follow in our path. Each of us fashioned our own success pattern, and we were among that select group of African American educators who had achieved success. Perhaps our pattern could be fashioned into a professional development program for other "dreamers." Surely, we had lessons that we could pass on to others. Just as Luther Foster gave me the benefit of lessons that he had learned, we were all convinced that we could replicate that pattern and practice.

We stood on the shoulders of very special educational leaders; now it was time for us to offer our shoulders and hands for others to stand on and grasp—if they had the dream to be where we were. So it was that we had the audacious idea to form the President's Round Table. Just as I had been thrust into the leadership role to form another professional organization (the National Association of College Auxiliary Services as a founder), so it was that Chuck Green became the first convener of the President's Round Table. Our dreams were coming to fruition. We began to take outstanding men and women under our individual wings, and they began to populate senior leadership ranks.

The seeds of the initial dream served as fertilizer for the Thomas Lakin Institute for Mentored Leadership to be conceived and crafted by Dr. Belle Wheelan. The record is clear that more presidents of color have been selected into the halls of the college presidency as a result of their participation in the development programs of the President's Round Table. The growth and breadth of the Round Table continues with the annual Men of Color Institute—new dreams are being realized as needs emerge.

We pioneers can be rightfully described as "icons" or "fathers of a movement." However, we can proudly proclaim that there is a strong band of apostles that follow us who are also "dreamers."

I trust that this personal experience will be helpful as you follow my advice and write down your own bold ideas and dreams. Take care and keep on being outstanding students!

DARE TO FOLLOW YOUR DREAMS

A n individual approached former Senator Bill Bradley and asked if he really liked playing basketball. His response was "Yes, more than anything else I could be doing now."

The man then explained why he asked the question. "Years ago, I once played the trumpet. I played in a little band. We were rather good. We would play on weekends at colleges. In my last year, our little group had an offer to tour and make records. Everyone in the group wanted to, except me."

Bradley was asked why he chose not to continue playing with the group. He replied, "My father thought it was not secure enough. I guess I agreed. A musician's life is so transient. You are always on the road. No sureness that you will get your next job. It just did not fit into a life plan that I envisioned. So I went to law school, and I quit playing the trumpet, except for every once in a while.

Now I am so busy with other things in life that I don't have time."

Bradley was asked, "Do you enjoy the law?"

He replied, "It's okay. But it is nothing like playing the trumpet."

That exchange between Senator Bradley and an unnamed man prompts me to offer sage bits of advice. Always dare to follow your dreams. You see, how sad it is that Senator Bradley, and many like him, choose to shortchange themselves by engaging in occupations and activities that may be safe, conventional, and rewarding—but do not deliver any satisfaction, fulfillment, and joy in living.

Katina Kefalos observes that "The only real failure in life is failing to move in the direction of your dreams." Dr. Benjamin Mays wisely asserted that "To miss your dreams is not failure; having no dreams to reach for, that is the real failure."

Growing up, we all have dreams, hopes, and aspirations for ourselves. Unfortunately, various social, emotional, and practical pressures conspire to create fear, uncertainty, and self-doubt. The sad result is that our glorious dreams and hopes for ourselves are forced into the background. I want to share five ways to fend off fear, tap into your inner passion, and follow your dreams.

- Let your intuition lead you.
- Practice the art of creative visualization.
- Challenge your assumptions.
- Dare to go where no one else has gone.
- Tell yourself, "I can remake my life."

Let Your Intuition Lead You

Your intuition is a valid source of information. Learn to listen and trust that inner voice when it calls you to act. Explore the possibilities and take appropriate steps. An intuitive step led Suzanne Kind to become a member of the US Olympic cross-country ski team in 1994. "I started training and ski racing when I was twenty-two. Almost a decade later than most athletes," she states. Newly married and living in Marquette, Michigan, she began cross-country skiing and racing. At the end of the first season, she placed fourth at one of the national collegiate championships in the women's 10K race. Then she began winning ever larger competitions.

The following year, she felt that she was within realistic reach of making the 1994 Olympic team. But now she questioned the legitimacy of that goal. She thought, "I'm just a ski bum, what is going to come of all of this?"

"Yet all the while, my intuition told me that this was okay, and over time, I began to accept my decision as valid and worthwhile."

She made the US Olympic team in both 1994 and 1998.

"Now I teach others, so I have turned my passion into an ongoing pursuit."

This came about because she let her intuition lead her. What about you?

Practice Creative Visualization

This simple but powerful process is described thusly. "In creative visualization, you use your imagination to create a clear image of something you wish to manifest. Then you continue to focus on the idea or picture regularly, giving positive energy until it becomes objective reality . . . In other words, until you actually achieve that which you have been visualizing" (Shakti Gawain, author of *Creative Visualization*).

An individual who knew how to use such visualization was legendary hotelier Conrad Hilton. The Great Depression was exceptionally hard for Hilton. After the economic crash of 1929, people did not travel much and, when they did, they were not staying in the hotels Hilton had acquired during the roaring 1920s. Business at his hotels was so poor that by 1931 his creditors were threatening to foreclose on his properties. He was so financially destitute that even his laundry was in hock, and he was borrowing money from the bellboy in order to eat. Conrad Hilton came upon a photograph of the Waldorf Astoria Hotel with its six kitchens, two hundred cooks, five hundred waiters, two thousand rooms, its private hospital, and private railroad siding in the basement. Hilton clipped that photograph out of the magazine and scribbled across it: "The greatest of them all."

The year 1931 was a "presumptuous, an outrageous time to dream," Hilton later wrote. Nevertheless, he put the photo of the Waldorf in his wallet, and when he had a desk again, slipped the picture under the glass top. That magazine photo was always in front of him. As he worked his way back up, he slipped the cherished photo under the glass of a new, larger desk. Eighteen years later, in October 1949, Conrad Hilton acquired the Waldorf Astoria Hotel.

The lesson to be learned from Conrad Hilton is this: "Conceive in order to achieve the life you want. Develop a mental picture of what you hope to accomplish. Have something for your mind to focus on, and it will become a cue for your behavior. As Rev. Jesse Jackson always states in his speeches, "If you can conceive it—believe it."

Challenge Your Assumptions

Many of us operate on flawed assumptions. We mistakenly assume that we cannot do more, be more, or enjoy more. Challenge your assumptions in order to rise above them. When I was the first person in my family to attend and graduate from college, I had the dream of one day being a college business manager—but not the first ever African American president of a college in the SUNY system, and the first African American chancellor of the Dallas County Community College District.

But somewhere along the way, I was caused to believe in me! I challenged those early assumptions! Now, I truly believe that there is nothing that I cannot accomplish!

Dare to Go Where No One Else Has Gone

Be challenged by the impossible. Be the nonconformist in your group. Take a chance. Embrace a risky task. Always be bold enough to try something really big. But keep this in mind that you'll have to do it, as I have—bit by bit, one step at a time. But you can do it!

Tell Yourself: "I Can Remake My Life"

You have the power to shape your destiny because destiny is more a matter of choice than of change. Choose to remake your life if you are feeling unfulfilled or unhappy. Consider the example set by Sheryl Draker. As an attorney in a Dallas law firm, she felt uneasy about leaving work early to see a doctor about a persistent stomach problem. After a medical exam, Draker was alarmed to hear she had a pancreatic tumor. Three days later, she arrived at a hospital for surgery only to learn that the doctors could not find the tumor. "I don't know whether it was a medical error or a miracle, but I took it as a wake-up call," she says. "The message was clear to me that I was not living the life I loved."

She quit her job with the corporate law firm and began working as a contract lawyer, similar to being a temporary employee. That allowed her to study for a master's degree in psychology. Today, Draker is self-employed as a legal and communications consultant in Austin, Texas. Typically, she works no more than eighty hours a month, yet earns triple what she did as a lawyer working sixty-hour weeks. The extra time allows her to do volunteer work. She is enjoying life!

Finally, when working to making your dreams come true, always maintain an optimistic outlook and attitude. If the going gets a little tough, keep in mind this wisdom from the American philosopher William James: "It is our attitude at the beginning of a difficult undertaking which, more than anything else, will determine the outcome."

Charles Swindoll, the famed contemporary theologian, author, and educator, had this pithy statement as I close this piece: "Your attitude determines your altitude."

Dare to follow your dreams!

PART TWO

LESSONS IN LEADERSHIP

"Even if you are on the right road, you will get run over if you just sit there."
—Will Rogers

Opening the Hinges of the Leader's Toolbox
Flash Points—Leadership in Place
Set Yourself Up for Success at the Next Level
What It Takes to Make a Senior Team Great
Leadership Thoughts
Leadership Expressions of Wright Lassiter
The "How-to-Be" Leader—Going Forward
The Art of Leadership
The Nine Faces of Leadership
Mentoring Guidance
Thoughts on Adversity and Opportunity
The Hardest Person to Lead
How to Deal With Failure
Nine Truths of Community College Leadership
Forty Lessons Learned Over Four Decades
Appreciation Aids Motivation

LEADERSHIP EXPRESSIONS OF WRIGHT LASSITER

An Interview for Basic Leadership Participants

➢ *What is your broad view of leadership?* Leadership is ultimately about creating a way for people to contribute to making something extraordinary happen.

➢ *What are essential elements?* Vision, conviction, perseverance, fortitude, and the courage to take calculated risks.

➢ *Can you describe leadership more broadly?* Leadership is not the private reserve of a few charismatic men and women. It is a process that ordinary people use when they are bringing forth the best from themselves and others. I have a shorthand way of describing leadership. It is that leadership can be spelled in a unique way— INFLUENCE. Leaders are those who make extraordinary things happen by liberating the leader within everyone.

I have many books on leadership in my library. I like the one by Kouzes and Posner, *The Leadership Challenge.* In their book, they make the point that when getting extraordinary things done in organizations, leaders engage in five practices of exemplary leadership:

- Model the way
- Inspire a shared vision
- Challenge the process
- Encourage the heart

➢ *Do you have leadership practices that you have assimilated from your reading, teaching, and experience?* Let me try and recite some expressions that I both use in teaching and coaching, and that I try to model as a leader myself:

- Titles are granted, but it is behavior that wins respect.
- You must lead from what you believe.
- Deeds are far more important than words.
- Exemplary leaders always go first.
- Everything begins with a dream.
- The dream or the vision is the force that invents the future.
- To enlist people in a vision, leaders must know their constituents and always speak their language.
- Leaders must breathe life into hopes, dreams, and aspirations.
- Leaders must be in all places.
- Leaders venture out. They are pioneers. They are risk takers.
- Leaders are willing to step out into the unknown.
- Leaders have unquestioned faith.
- Innovation and change involve experimentation, risk, and failure. The leader must encourage those attributes.
- The key that unlocks the door to opportunity is learning. Leaders are continual learners. They never stop seeking. Curiosity is their life preserver.
- Great dreamers don't become significant realities through the actions of a single person. Leadership is a team effort. Exemplary leaders make it possible for others to do good work.

➢ *You say that you practice encouraging the heart; can you say more about that?* Leaders must encourage the heart because the journey is often difficult and challenging. It is part of the leader's job to show appreciation for the contributions of others and to create a culture of celebration and collaboration.

Let me expand on that point with a couple of closing offerings. Celebrations and recognitions are always about fun and games; there is a definite place for that. However, for the leader, it is how he/she both tangibly and behaviorally link rewards with performance. My closing point is that leadership is a relationship between those who aspire to lead and those who choose to follow.

Thank you for the opportunity to share these thoughts with you for the class project.

THE "HOW-TO-BE" LEADER GOING FORWARD

Once again, I am pleased to address the participants in the Basic Leadership Program. As I have spoken to previous classes, you may have noted some prior comments of mine. First, we lead by example. As a leader, everything that we say or do sends a message, sets a tone, or teaches what to do and not to do. *Leadership* is a word that we toss around often in our conversations. We refer to "world-class" leaders, leaders for the new era, and the leaders of tomorrow.

Today's presentation is designed to provide just a few concepts on leadership techniques that will enable the leader, or the prospective leader, to operate in what is called the fourth level of change—the success zone.

The writer for a business periodical asked a number of corporate executives to "look over the horizon of today's headlines, size up the future, and describe the pressing tasks that lie beyond the millennium for executives." As I reviewed their responses, they appear to have broad application. I applied the same assignment to my graduate students at Dallas Baptist University, and I also gave my input on what I saw in the future. I offer these suggestions for your consideration as you begin the Basic Leadership Program for this year.

➤ The three major challenges facing leaders today, and for the future, have little to do with managing the enterprise's tangible assets, and everything to do with monitoring the quality of leadership, the workforce, and relationships.
➤ The leader beyond the millennium will not be the leader who has learned the lessons of "how to do it," with ledgers of "hows" balanced with "its" that dissolve in the crashing of changes ahead. The leader

for today and the future will be focused on HOW TO BE. How to develop quality, character, mind-set, value, principles, and courage.

➢ The "how-to-be" leader knows that people are the organization's greatest asset.

➢ The "how-to-be" leader builds dispersed and diverse leadership. That leader distributes leadership to the outermost edges of the circle to unleash the power of shared responsibility.

➢ The "how-to-be" leader long ago banned the hierarchy and involving many heads and hands, built a new kind of structure.

➢ The new design took people out of the boxes of the old hierarchy and moved them into a more circular, flexible, and fluid management system that spawned liberation of human spirit and endeavor.

➢ The "how-to-be" leader holds forth the vision of the organization's future that ignites the spark needed to build the inclusive enterprise.

➢ The "how-to-be" leader knows that listening to the customer and learning what he or she values—"digging in the field"—will be a crucial component, even more so in the future than today.

➢ The "how-to-be" leader—whether he or she is working in the private, public, or social sector—recognizes the significance of the lives of the men and women who make up the enterprise, and the value of a workplace that nurtures the people as critical to the success of the organization.

➢ The first principle of leadership is that it is a relationship between a leader and the followers. Without followers, there is no one to lead.

➢ Effective leaders are aware of and consciously manage the dynamics of the leader-follower relationship.

➢ The leader is at the center of a number of forces, each with its own agenda. These forces demand that the leader behave in ways and patterns that further their goals.

➢ Leaders in the twenty-first century will face greater and more complex demands than they in the previous century. Until recently, leaders had the power to shape their organizations in ways that supported their personal values, assumptions, and style. A variety of internal and external factors, pressures, and demands have all eroded the autonomy of the previous organizational leader.

➤ Effective leaders for the new millennium will hold certain traits in common:

- High ego strength.
- The ability to think strategically.
- An orientation to the future.
- A belief in certain fundamental principles of human behavior.
- Strong convictions and do not hesitate to display them.
- Politically astute.
- The ability to use power both for efficiency and the larger good as they see it.
- Emphatic—in that they have the ability to "get into the heads" of others with whom they relate.
- A persona determined by strong values and a belief in the capacity of individuals to grow.
- An image of the society in which they would like their organizations and themselves to live.
- Visionary.

In short, the "how-to-be" leader will believe strongly that they can help to shape the organization for the future. They will act on their beliefs through their personal behavior. Hopefully, these observations, from my perspective, will be helpful to you in this program and in your individual personal and professional lives. Be strong students at all times!

MENTORING GUIDANCE

Being able to talk about your work and your career plans with an experienced executive can be beneficial. Mentors can help you see things in a way that you might not have thought about. They have all been there many times before, often under diverse and challenging circumstances. It is no news flash, of course, that there is value in the relationship between a mentor and a "mentee." Finding a mentor is usually an informal affair. Often, mentorships develop between junior- and senior-level employees in the same organization.

I can say with humbleness and modesty that I am viewed as a highly successful individual. As a consequence, I am often approached by individuals and asked to be their mentor. Whenever an individual uses the word "mentor," I ask them to research the origin of the word, for it is a word that goes far back into ages past. It is not a relationship where one asks another to be a mentor, unless a relationship has been established—usually as a result of close observation (role model viewing), or direct and indirect interactions in the work setting. It generally results from interactions and associations that reach a point where the superior individual approaches the "seeker" and suggests a deeper relationship.

To the uninformed (and often inexperienced) individual, my comments about the nature and function of mentorship can be quite alarming and unsettling. The typical response is "I never thought of it that way." A personal experience in this area is often helpful in the conversation.

I have had very few "mentors," but I have had prominent role models that I fashioned my life and work after. One such individual (the president of Tuskegee Institute) reached the point with me where I viewed him as a mentor. It was late in my career, not early. He was a prominent role model in that I adopted his methods, style, and practices. No interactions—just keen observation. There were infrequent interactions, always at his initiative; however, valuable guidance was always imparted. These examples of the infrequent interactions and lessons learned proved helpful to me.

Tuskegee Institute was forty miles from the nearest airport. Tuskegee had a board of trustees of national figures who traveled by air to board meetings. Someone had to go to the airport and serve as the driver for the trustee. When the president asked you to serve as a "trustee driver," you knew that you had attracted his attention. On the day of the assignment, you would visit him in his office and he would give these instructions: "Have your car immaculate, be on time, and be prepared to engage in meaningful conversation with the trustee over the course of the forty-mile trip. Thank you and be on your way."

My first passenger was the chairman of the board of General Motors. What do you say to the head of what was then the largest corporation in America? He made it easy by initiating the conversation when he asked, "Outside of your normal job assignments, is there anything else that you do?" At the time, I was serving as chairman of the board of directors of the Tuskegee Industrial Development Corporation. He then asked, "Do you have any projects on the drawing board?" At the time, we were exploring the prospects of bringing to Tuskegee a facility to produce tomatoes in hothouses. It was called the "hydroponic process." His response was "That is interesting. I have had some research done on the finances associated with that process." For the balance of the trip to Tuskegee and the return to the airport at the conclusion of the board meeting, and for the next six months, he and I would exchange notes on that process. That was a powerful result of how a "mentor" had an influence in my life.

It was the advice of Dr. Foster that guided me when I reached the point where I had been approached regarding having my name placed in nomination for a college presidency. I had departed Tuskegee and become the chief financial and management officer at Morgan State University. He and I had a fifteen-minute telephone conversation, after which I chose to not have my name placed in nomination. Based on his counsel, it was two and a half years later when I concluded that I was "ready." I applied for the presidency of Schenectady County Community College in Schenectady, New York. To the surprise of many, I was selected as a president in my first attempt. I attribute that success to the relationship that I had with a mentor and just two telephone conversations.

I have thirteen direct reports as chancellor. While I have close relationships with all of them, there are five that I work with more closely than the others in a mentor/protégé relationship. I was the initiator in each case.

There is one individual in our organization, outside of my direct reports, that I have a special coaching relationship with. It started when he began pursuing his doctorate and has continued to the point where he is actively seeking a presidency. Based on his "package" and our relationship, I am confident that in time he will be successful.

An individual at one of the colleges in our organization called and asked me to be his mentor. I knew him by name only. This was my response. "With my impending retirement and the fact that you and I do not have a relationship based on your role there, mentoring would be problematic under the best of circumstances. However, I can be helpful to you in suggesting reading materials and other actions along those lines. Careful reading of my weekly commentary in The Weekend Memo should also prove to be beneficial. Let me know what your career goals are: that would be helpful if we should have future chances to talk." This "mentoring guidance" may be helpful to others.

THOUGHTS ON ADVERSITY
AND OPPORTUNITY

- ➢ Adversity introduces a person to himself.
- ➢ Touch a thistle timidly and it pricks you, grasp it boldly and its spikes crumble.
- ➢ Most people find that success is built and discovered out of adversity of some kind.
- ➢ How we react to problems determines not only our degree of growth and maturity, but our future success. It is reaction that determines the result.
- ➢ We can change circumstance by the certain stance of our souls. We must first adapt—then adjust—and then ADVANCE.
- ➢ Opportunity beckons more assuredly when misfortune comes upon a person than it ever does when a person is riding the crest of a wave of success.
- ➢ "The people who get on in this world are the people who get up and look for the circumstances they want, and if they can't find them— make them!" (George Bernard Shaw)
- ➢ "On the occasion of every accident that befalls you, ask yourself and inquire what power you have for turning it to use, or advantage." (Epictetus)

THE HARDEST
PERSON TO LEAD

I t does not take one long to realize that leadership is hard. You should be able to conjure up the names of at least half a dozen people who make that a true statement. All kinds of things make leadership difficult, but certain people are one of these.

As the picture of certain people comes to mind, take a minute to let that picture fade. Because of all the difficult people you will lead, the hardest person to lead will be yourself.

Call it what you want—the discipline of a leader, self-leadership, managing yourself—you have got your work cut out for you. The journey of leadership is as much inward as it is outward. Leadership, done well, will continually be a force that drives you back into the center of yourself to find out what you are really made of. Great leadership occurs when you understand your own motives, your "dark side," what you want to misrepresent in order to look better than you really are.

One of the things that I believe deeply is this: Leaders ought to be the most self-aware people in the room. I am not talking about a narcissistic self-awareness. You know those kinds of persons who only know two pronouns: *I* and *me*. No, not that kind of self-awareness.

I am talking about the kind of self-awareness that makes you comfortable in your own skin. You know who you are and who you are not. You lean into and lead out of your strengths. You have the words for your brokenness, and while you may wish you had none, you know that you do and you know what they are. And you know that other people know. You would not have it any other way. People like that are strong and lovely. Are you one of them?

Good leaders lead well for sake of themselves. We must possess a deep level of insight into who we are and why. In order to lead out of good motives, we need to be aware of our blind spots and lead for the good of others, rather than filling some void in ourselves.

Good leaders also lead well for the sake of others. A significant part of leadership is helping others function out of that centered place, and the best person to lead us there is someone who has already traveled that difficult road.

This brings us to the tough part. Why is it that so many leaders lack self-awareness? Because it's hard. Some of the hardest work you will ever do. The difficult inner journey.

And because it is hard and on the inside, sometimes we just don't do it. It is easier to simply cover it up with outside stuff that looks impressive, burying the soul under a heap of life's rubble.

Here is the paragraph where I write what you already know. Eventually, avoidance will catch up with you, so you might as well pay attention now. If you don't, it is only a matter of time before you will be exposed for the empty, hollow shell that you are. Please know that I am not accusing anyone; I am only making a cogent point. The outside will get stripped away, and the big reveal will show that your motives and ego were bigger than your leadership. And you will crumble. Maybe.

What I have said is possible, and we've all been spectators of that unraveling without having to buy any tickets. But it is also possible to keep on living and leading out of a hollow and selfish center, and do it until you die or are no longer in a leadership role.

There are lots of reasons to lead yourself well: so you don't get caught, so your influence won't disintegrate, so you won't lie on your deathbed with overwhelming regrets. But none of these are reasons enough. Only authenticity will. Good leadership is about what is real and right.

Readers of this book will note that I am an ordained Baptist minister. I want to now move into that arena with a few snippets of note.

Like so many things, self-awareness comes down to the bedrock of God. Can we trust him? Is he good? Answer those two questions and you will be a long way down the road of that inner journey.

Leading yourself is largely about living a rhythm of life that renews the life of God in us. It is about being utterly convinced of his goodness. It is about passion and energy and the joy that comes out of that center.

Leadership that is built on the bedrock of God is about a lot more than "quiet time." Sometimes quiet time is nothing more than a rule by which we measure whether or not we are good enough.

Leaders who are appropriately connected to the reality of their brokenness and the gift of God's forgiveness are able to easily utter the words that build community: "I'm sorry." Great leaders say it authentically and often. It is impossible for people who sin to build relationships and not have to apologize on a regular basis. Too often, our pride has us choking on those two little words.

Here is one final thought on leading yourself. There is a profound passage in John 16. In this Scripture, Jesus has made it clear to His disciples that his death is imminent. In addition, he has told them that in the face of that, they will soon abandon him. "You will leave me alone," he tells them.

Leaders often say that leadership is lonely. Jesus said that kind of aloneness makes you realize that God is always there. There is a difference between being left alone and being without a Presence. There will come a day that isn't about your leadership at all, the day when you find that your final breath is near. That is the main point of self-leadership—a life spent fighting and connecting for the greater good and not selfish ends.

HOW TO DEAL
WITH FAILURE

I t is often said that "failure is not an option." That is not a belief that I embrace. I will submit to you that if we are truly honest, failure does occur in our lives, sometimes in spite of our best efforts. A more appropriate adage might be "quitting or giving up is not an option." Because to quit or give up is to put a permanent stamp on a temporary situation, which is what failure really is—a temporary situation.

So much of the good in our world is due to people who did not give up. Imagine what our world would be missing if Thomas Edison had given up after his first unsuccessful experiment in making the electric lightbulb. The story goes that Edison and his assistants had tried 9,900 times when one assistant said to him, "Let's give up, we have failed 9,900 times." Edison responded, "We have not failed. We have had 9,900 opportunities."

It was after attempt number forty-five thousand that they finally created the lightbulb. How landlocked we would be if Wilbur and Orville Wright had given up after their first failed attempt at flight. Imagine how backward we would be if Dr. Martin Luther King Jr. had given up after he was told his "dream" was impossible. Imagine the nonexistence of this country if George Washington had given up. You will recall that he had every reason to give up and quit; for he and his troops had lost many battles—except the last one.

Every wonderful invention, every positive belief turned into positive action, is the direct result of someone who did not give up. Everyone is going to fail once in a while, no matter how hard you try not to. Show me someone who has not failed, and you have shown me someone who has not tried anything. The important thing is how you respond when failure occurs. Winners in life do several things.

First, winners see failure as normal. Basketball fans may remember these comments by Michael Jordan: "I've missed more than nine thousand shots in my life. I have lost more than three hundred games. Thirty-six times, I've been trusted to take the game-winning shot, and I missed. I have failed over and over again in my life. And that is why I succeed!" He was saying in essence, "It's okay to fail. It is not okay to give up."

Second, winners see the positive value of failure. Winners learn from their failure, apply their learning, and get better the next time around. I once read that "failure is only feedback, and feedback is a blessing." Conversely, when losers fail, they just give up. A museum director once said, "My grandpa always used to say that falling on your face is the first step forward." Don't make the mistake of despairing failure. Handled properly, it could be your surest ticket to success. It is a mistake to assume people succeed through success—more often than not, they succeed through failures. Precept, study, advice, and example sometimes cannot teach as well as what you learn from your failures.

Winners throw away their failures, but keep the lessons learned from them. Maybe you have learned to be more visible at work, as you have a better chance of getting a future promotion. You have learned to work harder on what we call the "soft dimension," which is fostering relationships. Maybe you have learned to control your temper so you don't blow the next relationship.

Lessons learned from failure are gifts. Resolve from this day forward that when you experience failure, you will take time to discover its lesson. The lessons will always be there; do not miss them because they are critical.

Thomas Watson Sr., the founder of IBM, affirmed that. When he was asked the quickest way to success, he said, "Double your failure rate."

Life is a series of ongoing experiences. Our role is to recognize this and to live our lives, professionally and personally, in a reflective manner that allows us to make the necessary changes to revolve into better versions of ourselves. Ponder my personal checklist:

- Use the experiences of daily living to grow personally and professionally.
- Problems are opportunities in disguise.
- Clouds do have silver linings.

- Life's lessons can be learned the hard way or the easy way.
- Use the weaknesses within your strengths to understand life lessons.
- Mastery of each life lesson opens a gateway to the next.
- Endings create the opportunity for new beginnings.
- Take stock of your life, assess what you have learned from your failures, and put those lessons to good use.

NINE TRUTHS OF COMMUNITY COLLEGE LEADERSHIP

1. Every decision you make has three elements: educational, fiscal, and political. Too often, we are good on the first element, and not on the other two. I have heard it too often: "I'm an educator, not a politician." Wrong thinking.
2. No CEO ever got fired for having a lousy curriculum, but many have been fired for not balancing the books. Seventy-five to eighty-five percent of our budgets is personnel. All members of the senior team must understand budgeting. If you cannot pay the bills, you are gone.
3. Change is stressful and threatening, and you will be resisted from time to time. Occasionally, you, as a leader, must walk the path of most resistance and do what is right and needed.
4. Organizational conspirators are alive and well. And some of them are wearing the same color jersey as you.
5. Leadership and management are different skills. We have never heard anyone say that Winston Churchill was a great manager, but he was a great leader.
6. There are three sides to every coin. Our job as administrators and leaders is to clarify the ambiguity that dominates so many aspects of human behavior and our organizations. If you can't deal with ambiguity, avoid the leadership business.
7. Leaders must be self-starters. If you are looking for a lot of praise, you are in the wrong business. Besides, the people who come up and pat you on the back may be trying to stab you.

8. There are no secrets in a bureaucracy. This is a hard one for many to understand. Always give your staff the full deck of fifty-two cards. Just don't tell them what the trump card is.
9. Not all rocks are meant to be turned over. If you are the leader, every problem is your problem. But not all problems are meant to be tackled by you. Cut yourself some slack—let some of the other team members get in the fray first.

FORTY LESSONS LEARNED OVER FOUR DECADES

1. Learn to say "I don't know." If used when appropriate, it will be used often.
2. It is easier to get into something than to get out of it.
3. If you are not criticized, you may not be doing much.
4. Look for what is missing. Many know how to improve what's there; few can see what isn't.
5. It is easier to identify a leader from his/her back than to see him/her coming.
6. Work for a boss to whom you can tell it like it is. Remember, you cannot pick your family, but you can pick your boss.
7. Constantly review developments to make sure that the actual benefits are what they were supposed to be. Avoid Newton's Law.
8. Good leaders must be wise enough to differentiate a fad from a genuine winner.
9. Celebrate accomplishments and never tackle your teammates.
10. However menial and trivial your early assignments may appear, give them your best effort—that will pay dividends in the future.
11. Effective leaders understand that the use of data leads to good decision-making.
12. Persistence or tenacity is the disposition to persevere in spite of difficulties, discouragement, or indifference. Do not be known as a good starter but a poor finisher.
13. Don't try the same programs and expect new results.
14. Confirm the instructions you give others, and their commitments in writing. Never assume that it will get done.
15. Practice shows that those who speak the most knowingly and confidently often end up with the assignment to get the job done.

16. Strive for brevity and clarity in oral and written reports.
17. Be extremely careful in the accuracy of your statements.
18. Learn to keep an open mind and let others share their opinions. In short—listen, listen, and listen.
19. Always make communication a priority.
20. Never overlook the fact that, even as a leader, you are working for someone. Keep him or her, or the board, informed. Whatever the boss wants, within the bounds of integrity, always takes top priority.
21. Promises, schedules, and estimates are important instruments in a well-run organization.
22. Never direct a complaint to the top. A serious offense is to "cc" a person's boss on a copy of a complaint before the person has a chance to respond to the complaint.
23. When communicating with someone outside the organization, remember that you are always representing your organization. Be mindful always of your commitments.
24. Cultivate the habit of boiling matters down to the simplest terms. The proverbial "elevator speech" is a proven best practice.
25. Cultivate the habit of making a quick, clear-cut decision.
26. When making decisions, the "pros" are much easier to deal with than the "cons." However, your boss wants to see both.
27. Do not ever lose your sense of humor.
28. Do not make expedient decisions that have long-term effects.
29. Have fun at what you do. It will be reflected in your work. No one likes a group except another group!
30. Treat the name of your organization as if it were your own.
31. Beg for the bad news.
32. You can never polish a sneaker.
33. When facing issues or problems that are becoming drawn out, "short them to the ground."
34. When faced with decisions, try to look at them as if you were one level up in the organization. Your perspective may change quickly.
35. A person who is nice to you but rude to the waiter, or to others, is not a nice person. This rule never fails.
36. Never be afraid to try something new. Remember an amateur built an ark that survived a flood, while a large group of professionals built the *Titanic*.
37. The qualities of leadership boil down to confidence, dedication, integrity, and love.

38. Have courage. One of the most important characteristics for great leadership is courage at the helm.
39. Hire great people and support professional development.
40. Minimize the number of your enemies. Don't make enemies if you don't have to.

APPRECIATION AIDS MOTIVATION

In one of my reading sources, this quotation caught my attention: "It is not enough anymore to merely satisfy your customer. Customers must be delighted—surprised by having their needs not just met, but exceeded." That, in my opinion, is the essence of customer service, irrespective of the industry.

Serving customers (in higher education students and other stakeholders) are two words that cover so much. What is involved? Answering questions. Solving problems. Untangling logjams. Fixing what's broken and finding what's lost. Soothing the irate and reassuring the timid. The whole gamut. Time after time, excellent customer service means performing the business equivalent of pulling a rabbit out of a hat. Does that sound familiar?

In the 1980s, professional business watchers began to notice something important—not to mention surprising. Those few organizations that had dedicated themselves to working hard at giving their customers superior service were producing better results. They also started to notice that successful service organizations had lower costs, fewer upset and complaining customers, and more repeat business. Customers were voting with their feet and beating a path back to the doors of the companies that served them well. What's more, good service also had internal rewards in lower employee turnover and absenteeism, higher morale, and job satisfaction.

Almost overnight, being customer focused, understanding and meeting customer needs, coddling customers with TLC, and giving quality customer service became a critical organizational goal and received spotlight attention. Books were written, banners hung, and speeches made, all trumpeting the importance of high-quality customer service. A revolution in the way customer service was viewed and valued began, and continues to this day.

There is an unbroken rule that should never be forgotten as far as the customer is concerned—YOU the company; the college; the business. Whether customers' feelings about an organization are good or bad often relates directly to the experience with one member of that organization. Their attitude is clear: "Help me with this issue or question please." Customer relations is an integral part of everyone's job—not an extension or add-on.

Today's customers are demanding, and they have every right to be. Today's customers have more options than ever before. If your institution does not offer what they want or need, if you do not interact with them in a manner that meets or exceeds their expectations, they will just walk away and do "business" with a competitor. Losing customers can result in losing jobs.

I am frequently asked to share my views on what constitutes good customer service. First, it must be reliable. Reliability means keeping the Service Promise. That is, doing what you say you do to and for the customer.

Second, it is responsive. Timeliness has always been important. And today, responsive action—doing things, keeping commitments in a timely fashion—is even more crucial. The best time for anything is the time that is best for the customer. But dissatisfaction is not measured in minutes. Rather, dissatisfaction is often the result of uncertainty. Research shows that the most frustrating aspect of waiting is not knowing how long the wait will be.

Third, excellent customer service is reassuring. Today's customer service professionals know there is much more involved in creating customer satisfaction than smiles and happy faces. If being nice was the answer, good service would be the norm; but that is clearly not the case. Make no mistake—courtesy, good manners, and civility is important. Treat your customers like dirt, or that they don't matter, and they will make your life miserable every time. Keep in mind that courtesy is not a substitute for competence and skill. You want your customers to know that they can trust you because of the competence and confidence that you display.

Fourth, excellent or superior customer service is empathetic. Customers come to the service setting with a wide variety of shapes and sizes. They bring an equally wide variety of wants, needs, expectations, attitudes, and emotions. Consequently, customers want to be treated as individuals. No one likes to be treated like a number by a service-staff member responding like a machine. When you recognize your customers' emotional state, that helps you figure out the best way to effectively and professionally serve them.

Now there will be times when emotions will run high, especially when things have gone wrong for the customer. It is easy to get caught up in a customer's emotional world. Keep in mind that when responding to the emotions of a customer, it is helpful make a distinction between empathy and sympathy. Both have to do with how you respond to other people's emotions. The two terms should not be used interchangeably. They are different, and the difference is important.

Sympathy involves identifying with, and even taking on, another person's emotions. A sympathetic response is "I'm really angry about this situation, just as you are."

Empathy means acknowledging and affirming another's emotional state. An empathetic response is "I can understand how that makes you angry."

Responding to customers with sympathy puts you on an emotional roller coaster and can leave you worn out and frazzled at the end of the day. The trick is to be emotionally aware and sensitive without becoming too emotionally involved yourself. When you respond with empathy, you stay calm and in control. Only then are you at your absolute best: ready, willing, and able to help the customer. Showing empathy allows you to be professional and caring at the same time. It also makes the customer feel important.

Fifth, and finally, good customer service is tangible. Service is difficult to describe in tangible, physical terms. It is fuzzy, mushy—slippery. One of the major complications in providing service comes from the fact that so much of it is intangible. It is important to understand the role that tangibles play in making your intangible service memorable and satisfying. This example and I will be through. It is about going out to eat.

Before you enter a restaurant, you evaluate it based on some of its tangible attributes: advertising, location, cleanliness of the parking lot, smells, attendants, the facilities . . . is the sign lit and legible?

As you walk through the front door, you make more judgments. Is the hostess friendly? Is it clean? Can you find the restrooms without a guide? During your meal, you evaluate other tangibles. The menu. How was your order taken? The presentation of the food, and so forth.

After the meal, there are still more forms of tangible evidence for you to weigh. The friendliness of the wait service. The promptness in bringing the check and how that transaction was handled. Were there any suggestions made to encourage you to return? You know the drill here.

Tangibles help convey the value of the service transaction's intangible aspects. They are an important way for you to educate your customers and also help them evaluate the quality of the service that has just been provided. Manage the tangible aspects of the encounter well and you give your customers something solid to tie their impressions to.

The best rule of thumb regarding the tangibles you manage can be simply stated. Never give something to customers that you would be reluctant, embarrassed, or angry to receive yourself.

This was a presentation to the professional support staff at Mountain View College

PART THREE
THE SERVANT LEADER

"We are prone to judge success by the index of our
salaries or the sizes of our automobiles,
rather than by the quality of our service and relationship to society."
—Martin Luther King Jr.

The Servant Leadership Model

Leadership
Authority
Service
Love
Will

The Purpose of Life
My Life Is Not My Own
Questions I Ask Myself
Perspectives on Leadership
Who Is the Servant Leader?
The Serving Leader
The Characteristics of Effective, Caring Leaders
A Servant Leader's Journey: Experiences and Influences
Relationships Are a Measure of Stewardship
The Role of Personal Leadership
Leadership Is About the People for Whom We Are Responsible

THE PURPOSE OF LIFE

Several years ago, I came across a few paragraphs by an unnamed person that touched me deeply. The powerful thoughts contained in those few words may have utility for my readers.

"One day, when all of the employees reached the office, they saw a big note on the door on which it was written: 'Yesterday, the person who has been hindering your growth in this company passed away. We invite you to join the funeral in the room that has been prepared in the gymnasium.' They all felt sad for the death of one of their colleagues, but after a while, they got curious to know who this colleague was. The excitement in the gym was such that the security agents were ordered in to control the crowd within the room. Each of them wondered: 'Who is this guy who was hindering my progress? Well, at least he has died.' One by one, the curious employees got closer to the coffin; and when they looked inside it, each of them became speechless. They stood near the coffin, shocked and in total silence, as if someone had touched the deepest part of their soul. There was a mirror inside the coffin; everyone who looked inside it could see himself. There was also a sign next to the mirror that said: 'There is only one person who is capable to set limits on your growth; it is YOU!'

"You are the only person who can revolutionize your life. You are the only person who can influence your happiness, your goal realization, and your success. You are the only person who can help yourself. Your life does not change when your boss changes, your friends change, when your parents change, when your partner changes, or when your company changes. Your life changes when you change—when you go beyond your limiting beliefs, when you realize that you are the only one responsible for your life."

The most important relationship you can have is the one you have with yourself. Examine yourself and watch yourself. Do not be afraid of difficulties, impossibilities, and losses. Be a winner; build yourself and your reality. That is the way you face life so that you can make a difference.

The purpose of life is to live a life of purpose. These are interesting thoughts for reflection, and they can have relevance in your personal and professional life.

MY LIFE IS NOT MY OWN

I accept this prestigious award with the utmost humility and gratitude. It has been said that the failure to show and express gratitude ranks among the greatest of sins. It is in that spirit and context that I express thanks to President Cook and the Awards Committee for deeming me worthy of this award. I am truly humbled as I join the ranks of some of Dallas's most outstanding and extraordinary icons, leaders, and humanitarians.

I extend special words of thanks to the individuals who offered expressions on the video. You were most kind and generous with your words and assessment of what I may have contributed in the service of others.

Please applaud yourselves in this audience. Your presence here, first and foremost, represents your commitment to Dallas Baptist University and its mission to equip, empower, and encourage young people to go forth and also be of service.

When Dr. Martin Luther King Jr. stood in Oslo to receive the Nobel Peace Prize, he began by stating that the award was not his alone, but it was shared with many others who had supported and assisted him. He used the metaphor of the airplane in how the pilot and first officer have the responsibility for the safe travel of the passengers. However, there are many others who enable the aircraft to be able to fly. Persons who are unseen and sometimes invisible, but without them, air travel would not be possible.

He spoke of the staff and assistant who enabled him to go about his tasks. Persons that the public rarely saw. But without them, he could not have engaged in his important work.

The same is true of me. I want to acknowledge the members of my board of trustees who are here and who enable me to "be of service."

My staff and colleagues, many of whom are here tonight. I thank you individually and collectively for your support and encouragement.

I must also acknowledge my pastor—the Reverend Bryan L. Carter. I thank him for providing opportunities for me to serve the Lord through the Concord Church.

Now, special accolades are in order for my wife of fifty-two years, who has unselfishly helped me in so many ways. Without her support and encouragement, none of what you have heard would have been possible. Thank you, my sweet one. I want to also acknowledge my children, for they—along with my wife—had to witness periods of absence on my part. It is encouraging to me that they have followed, in their own ways, the path that they witnessed of their father.

None of this would have been possible without the values instilled in me by my beloved mother and father. I recall very vividly on a certain occasion that my father took me aside and said these words to me: "Junior, I want to give you a definition of service that I want you to embrace and make it a part of your life. Service is the rent that you pay for the space that you occupy on earth." He repeated it for emphasis. As I loved and admired my father, I took the words to heart and put in practice. Later, as I approached young adulthood, he took me aside again and repeated: "Junior, service is the rent that you pay for the space that you occupy on earth—and I want you to always live in a high-rent district." His words have served as a linchpin in my life.

One of my friends on the video spoke of me being an author. I have been privileged to author eight books, and I am working on several others. Let me close these acceptance remarks with several quotes from my book on servant leadership. I believe it was John Wesley who said:

- Do all the good you can,
- In all the ways you can,
- For all the people you can,
- In all of the places that you can,
- For as long as you can.

I would ask this audience to ponder these other expressions that appear in my book:

- Give bountifully—without thought of getting anything for yourself in return.
- The Lord gives to us that we may give to others.
- God has given me time, initiative, and energy. It is important to use those gifts to help others.
- A person lives as he invests himself in the lives of others. A man is immortal as he is useful. He lives as long as the thing in which he has invested lives.
- You can make a difference if you link your life to a worthy institution that will live on when you have gone.

My life is not my own; Lord, to you I belong.
Heartfelt thanks and God bless each of you richly.

QUESTIONS I ASK MYSELF

Because of the work that I engage in as a teacher/leader in both the spiritual and secular domains, I have become quite a fan of John C. Maxwell. He has quite an extensive and prolific publishing arm—InJoy, Inc. The firm produces his books, monographs, and other teaching materials. I was fascinated with the title of one of his recent books, *Questions I Ask Myself.* I was intrigued to such an extent that I used that title in a presentation that I will abstract in this selection.

Am I investing in myself? This is a personal growth question. Lifelong learners and aspiring senior leaders have a common set of characteristics:

- They develop a personal growth plan.
- They possess a teachable spirit.
- They invest in growth-oriented resources and relationships.
- They continually leave their comfort zone.
- They capture what they learn by applying their knowledge.
- They reflect on what they learn and turn experience into insight.
- They pass on what they learn to others.

Am I genuinely interested in others? This is a motive question. Leaders see before others see, and they see more than others see. Since some leaders figure it out first, they can be tempted to take advantage of others. Self-centered leaders manipulate when they move people for personal benefit. Mature leaders motivate by moving people for mutual benefit. They place what's best for others above themselves.

Am I doing what I love and loving what I do? This is a passion question. You will never fulfill your destiny doing work that you despise. You are nothing unless what you do is done from the heart. If you go to work only to cycle through rote processes and functions, then you are already effectively retired.

Am I investing my time with the right people? This is a relationship question. Most people can trace their successes and failures to the relationships in their lives. Be selective about whom you join with on the leadership journey. Choose companions with a commitment to personal growth, a healthy attitude, and high potential.

Am I staying in my strength zone? This is an effectiveness question. Effective leaders stop working on their weaknesses and diligently develop their strengths. You don't have to be a jack-of-all-trades. Delegation frees you to focus on what you can offer to your organization.

Am I taking others to a higher level? My success is determined by the seeds I sow, not the harvest I reap. My life mission should be to add value to leaders who will multiply value to others. Leaders add value to others rather than accumulate value for themselves. Dr. Martin Luther King Jr. said it best: "Life's most urgent question is 'what you are doing for others?'"

Am I taking care of today? This is a success question. The secret of your success is determined by your daily agenda. Are the habits in your life steering you toward success or simply frittering away your time? Be serious about making every day count.

Am I taking time to think? This is a leadership question. A minute of thought is greater than an hour of talk. Taking time to think allows you to live life purposefully. Do not let life's circumstances dictate your path or allow the expectations of others to determine your course. Be the author of your life by always working to clear your schedule for thinking time.

Am I developing leaders? This is a legacy question. The ultimate test for a leader is not whether he or she makes smart decisions and takes decisive action, but whether he or she teaches others to be leaders and builds an organization with sustainability.

Am I pleasing God? This is an eternity question. I like this statement by Maxwell: "In the light of history, our years are short and our days are few. Yet our lives have greater significance than we can imagine." As the Roman general Maximus exhorts his men in *Gladiator*, "What we do in life echoes in eternity." Live your life honorably and with a clear conscience before God and your fellow man. Focus your effort on worthwhile causes that will outlast your time on this planet.

Make a practice of asking those questions from time to time, particularly in your reflective moments.

PERSPECTIVES ON SERVANT LEADERSHIP

I had the privilege of being selected for the closing plenary session at the Seventeenth Annual International Conference of the Robert K. Greenleaf Center for Servant Leadership held in Dallas, Texas. This entry in the book is a brief abstract of my observations to the audience of more than 1,500 attendees. I began the talk with three brief quotations from the Greenleaf writings. In answering the question "who is the servant leader?"—Greenleaf offers the following cogent expressions.

"The servant leader is servant first. It begins with the natural feeling that one wants to serve—to serve first. Then conscious choice brings one to aspire to lead. The difference manifests itself in the care taken by the servant. First, to make sure that other people's highest priority needs are being served.

"The best test, and most difficult to administer, is this: 'Do those served grow as persons? Do they, while being served, become healthier, wiser, freer, more autonomous, more likely themselves to become servants? And what is the effect on the least privileged in society; will they benefit or, at least, not be further deprived?

"If a better society is to be built, one that is more just and more loving, one that provides greater creative opportunity for its people, then the most open course is to raise both the capacity to serve and the very performance as servant of existing major institutions by new regenerative forces operating within them"

Those three quotations were taken from two of his timeless works: *The Servant as Leader* and *The Institution as Servant*. I highly recommend them to anyone who professes to be an exponent of the concepts of servant leadership.

After the customary opening perspectives to establish connection, I used the following stories to begin my keynote.

Let me begin with an incident that involved Benjamin Zander, founder and conductor of the Boston Philharmonic Orchestra, in a performance before an assembly of business executives who were gathered for a conference on human resource and management issues. In observing his performance, one could conclude that the role of the orchestra conductor can be equated with that of the servant leader. Zander elaborated to the assembly his views regarding that of the conductor.

He shared a revelation that had come to him as he was conducting his orchestra. It happened many years into his successful career—a career that has seen his name on the covers of many music compact discs and long-playing albums (if you remember those 33 1/3 albums). As he stood in front of his orchestra with his baton raised, Zander suddenly realized that he, the conductor, made no sound. Yes, it was his picture on all those posters announcing the concerts—but by himself, he made no music.

The job of the conductor is to get the best music out of the musicians. His role is to coach, encourage, support, and occasionally push. But the conductor never makes a sound.

A similar lesson can be gleaned from the annals of military leadership preparation for the British Army. One of the first things that the British Army teaches its new lieutenants is that the officers eat last. Feed the troops first—in other words, young leaders should never forget that their first concern is the welfare of those they lead.

The question could be asked: how do those two examples—the orchestra conductor and the army lieutenant—relate to leadership, be it the global leader or the servant leader? Very simply, leadership is not about those of us in senior executive positions. It is not about perks, our feelings, our ego, or our span of control. It is always about the people for whom we are responsible. Along with the title of *leader* comes a very heavy load that is weighed down with the additional concern of cultural sensitivity. From my perspective, the good news is that the servant leader can be trained and developed. But before training can take effect, the leader-in-training must start with one essential attribute: the clear understanding that it is about everyone but you.

Are you ready for servant leadership? Just look behind you. Is anyone following? I can tell you now, if you still think leadership is all about you, then there will not be anyone following behind. Servant leadership is about the people for whom we are responsible.

Leaders must have more of an armor of confidence in facing the unknown—more than those who accept their leadership. The servant leader must also be persuasive. People grow taller when those who lead empathize, and when they are accepted for what they are. Even though their performance may be judged critically in terms of what they are capable of doing. Leaders who empathize and who fully accept those who go with them on this basis are more likely to be trusted.

It is my hope that these observations on servant leadership will prove to be useful to all who choose to follow this path.

WHO IS THE
SERVANT LEADER?

Servant leadership deals with the reality of power in everyday life—its legitimacy, the ethical restraints upon it, and the beneficial results that can be attained through the appropriate use of power. I recall an article in the *New York Times* that listed the ten characteristics of the servant leader:

- Listening
- Empathy
- Healing
- Awareness
- Persuasion
- Conceptualization
- Foresight
- Stewardship
- Commitment to the growth of people
- Building community

Robert Greenleaf is the acknowledged modern-day leading exponent of the concept of servant leadership. He had a number of small in length publications during his lifetime. Recently, a number of exponents of the beliefs of Greenleaf published *Seeker and Servant* from his private writings. The book focuses on his reflections on religious leadership.

What emerges from the volume is Greenleaf's belief that seeking, prophecy, and leading are interdependent qualities of a larger "whole"—servant leadership. The leader must be a seeker first. And the leader must "seek to seek" rather than "seek to find."

Trusting his/her intuition, the leader may discover "lost knowledge" (things known to earlier societies, but obscured to modern society) and, in articulating it, may attract other seekers. When this has happened, the leader appears prophetic to the other seekers. Operating from an awareness of the good that is possible in people, the leader can then "go ahead and show the way" toward that which is possible (which is Greenleaf's definition of leadership).

Greenleaf was known to teach through questions and silence, always avoiding prescriptions. He does offer a prescriptive definition of the qualities of those who can develop themselves, and other servant leaders:

- They are strong, able, well-prepared people.
- They know who they are and where they stand.
- They have a clear vision, a sense of direction.
- They have a great sustaining spirit with which to confront adversity.
- They have unqualified dedication to the mission to which they are committed.

Donna C. L. Prestwood and Paul A. Schumann Jr. authored the book *Innovate! Straight Path of Quality, Customer Delight, and Competitive Advantage.* In their book, they make the point that leadership is now in a state of mind, not a position. In this highly interactive age, we will find ourselves increasingly in situations that demand the exercise of our innate capability to lead. They make the point that "it is imperative that each of us bring up the leader within us. The path to leadership growth is one of personal growth. Bringing up the leader within requires an understanding of seven new principles of leadership."

- Know who you are.
- Let go of what you've got hold of.
- Learn your purpose.
- Live in the question.
- Learn the art of "barn raising."
- Give "it" away.
- Let the magic happen.

I address each of those elements in other portions of the book. However, the first principle is instructive—*Know who you are.* The caterpillar posed that question in *Alice's Adventures in Wonderland.* As leaders, we are now confronted with the same question. The decision to answer this question is the beginning of the journey to becoming a leader. We must understand what we know and what we don't know about ourselves. We must assess our resistance to and tolerance for the following: change, our fears, our preferences, and our skills and abilities. I challenge the reader to draw your own conclusions regarding the six other attributes.

THE SERVING LEADER

The principles of servant leadership are not easy to make a part of our personal and professional lives. However, it is achievable. Functioning as a servant leader surfaces the values of humility, patience, care for others, and forbearance. Those values are rather easily stated, but challenging to fully embrace and model. I have crafted five requirements of the servant leader that may be instructive for the aspiring or functioning serving leader.

Upend the pyramid of conventional management thinking. Serving leaders put themselves at the bottom of the pyramid and work to unleash the energy, excitement, and talents of the team, the business, and the community. You qualify to be first by putting other people first. You are in charge primarily to "charge up" others.

Run to great purpose. The serving leader runs to great purpose by holding out in front of their team, business, or community a "reason why" that is so big it requires and motivates the best effort of everyone. To do the most possible good, the serving leader strives for the impossible. Moreover, the serving leader sustains the self's greatest interest in pursuits beyond self-interest.

Raise the bar of expectations. This is accomplished by being highly selective in the choice of team leaders and by establishing high standards of performance. These actions build a culture of performance throughout the team, business, or community. To serve the many, you must first serve the few. The best reach-down is a challenging reach-up.

Blaze the trail. This is accomplished by teaching serving-leader principles and practices, and by removing obstacles to performance. These actions multiply the serving leader's impact by educating and activating tier after tier of leadership. To protect your values, you must give it all away. The biggest obstacle is the one that hinders someone else.

Build on strength. To address your weaknesses, focus on your strengths. You cannot become the best unless others do also. So build on strength by arranging each person in the team, the business, and the community to contribute what he or she is best at. This improves everyone's performance and solidifies teams by aligning the strengths of many people.

TEN CHARACTERISTICS OF A SERVANT LEADER

To conclude this section on servant leadership, I have distilled the work of a number of leading thinkers to craft ten characteristics of a servant leader. Many of today's most creative thinkers are writing and speaking about servant leadership as an emerging leadership paradigm for the new millennium. The list is long and slowly growing and includes James Autry, Warren Bennis, Peter Bock, John Carter, Stephen Covey, Max DePree, Joseph Jaworski, Margaret Wheatley, Danah Zolar, and L. C. Spears, to name but a few of today's cutting-edge leadership authors and advocates of servant leadership. I offer this distillation of thought into ten characteristics for the consideration of my readers.

1. **Listening**. Leaders have traditionally been valued for their communication and decision-making skills. Those two very important skills need to be reinforced by a deep commitment to listening intently to others. The servant leader seeks to identify the will of a group and helps to clarify that as he/she listens receptively to what is being said and unsaid. Processing then follows after listening.

2. **Empathy**. The servant leader strives to understand and empathizes with others. People need to be accepted and recognized for their special and unique spirits. The most successful servant leaders are those who have become skilled empathetic listeners.

3. **Healing.** One of the great strengths of servant leadership is the potential for healing one's self and one's relationship to others.

4. **Awareness.** General awareness, and especially self-awareness, strengthens the servant leader.
5. **Persuasion.** Another characteristic of servant leaders is a reliance on persuasion, rather than on one's positional authority in making decisions within an organization.
6. **Conceptualization.** Servant leaders seek to nurture their abilities to dream great dreams.
7. **Foresight.** Closely related to conceptualization, the ability to foresee the likely outcome of a situation is hard to define, but easier to identify. Foresight is a characteristic that enables the servant leader to understand the lessons from the past, the realities of the present, and the likely consequence of a decision for the future.
8. **Stewardship.** Servant eldership, like stewardship, assumes first and foremost a commitment to serving the needs of others. It also emphasizes the use of openness and persuasion, rather than control.
9. **Commitment to the growth of people.** The servant leader recognizes the tremendous responsibility to do everything in his or her power to nurture the personal and professional growth of employees and colleagues.
10. **Building community.** The servant leader senses that much has been lost in recent human history as a result of the shift from local communities to large institutions as the primary shaper of human lives. This awareness causes the servant elder to seek to identify some means of building community among those who work within a given institution.

Servant-leadership characteristics often occur naturally within many individuals, and like many natural tendencies, they can be enhanced through learning and practice. Servant leadership offers great hope for the future of creating better, more caring institutions.

A SERVANT LEADER'S JOURNEY: EXPERIENCES AND INFLUENCES

Leadership is about the people for whom we are responsible. "How do you spell leadership?" is a question that I pose to my graduate classes and also to new entrants into the leadership fray. It is not LEADERSHIP, but it is spelled INFLUENCE. The objective of servant leadership is to enhance individualism, while at the same time increasing teamwork. Servant leadership removes the perilous ego and encourages one to lead through ingenuity and resourcefulness. The servant leader understands the importance of being part of a team, practices humility, and has a strong and principled vision.

In his book *The Winner Within*, NBA legend Pat Riley offers some insights on the danger of compromising excellence by not being a committed team member. "Being a game player is a fiction some people use to excuse themselves from working as hard as they should. People who think they are game players are what coaches call 'floaters.' They float along on a cushion of talent, or sheer physical size and strength. They don't see what all the fuss over concentration, work ethic, and teamwork is all about. That is, until players of lesser talent start scoring in their face, quarter after quarter, simply because they are more in tune with their game."

Eventually, every team has to learn that excellence, like servant leadership, is not a destination. It is a process that must be continually improved on.

The Beginning of My Journey

How did my journey toward learning the concepts of servant leadership begin? How have I endeavored to not only embrace the concept, but to also empower, equip, and encourage others? How did my journey begin, and were there any defining moments? This is the way my journey began and had its roots.

I recall that, as a child, my father sat with me and gave me his definition of the word "service." He said, "Junior, service is the rent that you pay for the space that you occupy here on earth." I heard him but, at that point, obviously did not fully comprehend the meaning of his expression. He would restate it from time to time. Apparently, when he thought that I had begun to grasp the meaning, he added a postscript: "Junior, always strive to live in a high-rent district."

Those simple expressions from my late father and best friend have emboldened me throughout my life, as I always wanted to follow in the footsteps of my father.

Perhaps the first defining moment in my life occurred just a few hours after my undergraduate graduation. I was the first in my family to attend college. It was a happy day for the Lassiter family. As we basked in the warmth of the occasion on the lawn in front of the Oakland Chapel, the chairman of the business department approached me. He asked if I had a job for the summer. He knew that I was headed for advanced study in the fall.

Well, because my father was a bricklayer and contractor, I always "had a job" when I was not at the college. Knowing what was in store for me as I waited for the beginning of graduate studies, I replied by asking, "Do you have something in mind?" He said, "We would like for you to stay here and join the faculty for the summer session." I was taken aback and shocked, but I remembered all of the lessons gleaned from my father and replied, "If you have enough faith and confidence in me to think that I can teach effectively, I am enough of a risk-taker to say YES." My family was overjoyed and gladly helped me take my possessions to the bachelor faculty residence.

The next day, I went to receive my class assignments. I was green behind the ears and knew nothing about faculty loads, so I accepted a teaching assignment of three classes! Only a novice would have been so foolish. The classes were accounting principles, business communication, and shorthand (a forgotten art now). As I prepared to leave his office with my textbooks under my arms, the chairman said something else: "By the way, I have to be away for the entire summer to attend to my sick mother, and we have decided that you can also serve as the acting department head. You can do it. If you have any problems, just go see Dean White. Have a good time this summer."

The story does not end there. The next day, I show up for my first class: Accounting Principles I. I was "ready," for I had read the textbook and solved all the problems up through chapter 8 so that I would never be behind the class. I had to impress my students. As I placed my materials on the desk, I look up, and who should be seated in front of me but my favorite high school teacher, Mrs. Rosa Parrott. I was the only male student in the typing classes and had set the standard. What a challenge for a rookie teacher. At the end of the class, Mrs. Parrott came up to me and said, "Mr. Lassiter, you have been the best college teacher that I have had thus far at Alcorn College." My willingness to be a risk-taker had been affirmed.

Another defining moment occurred later after I had completed my MBA studies and had now embarked on the journey to become the CFO of a college or university. My supervisor, the chief business officer, sat with me one day and shared with me the concept of service that had been established by the founder of Tuskegee Institute—the famed and legendary icon Booker T. Washington.

He said, "Lassiter, we take great pride in the community of Tuskegee. This culture of pride started with Dr. Washington. So when we senior executives see an individual with promise and potential, we sit with them, as I am sitting with you. We tell that throughout the history of the Institute, we have encouraged faculty and staff to take an interest in the betterment of the community—that is to be of service in some venue. When that becomes a part of the pattern and culture, we thus contribute to the greater good. I want you to go out and identify an area where you can make a contribution. Come back and discuss it with me and I will support your endeavors, if we are in agreement. You will be free to devote time to that endeavor, even if it requires service during the normal workday. Your only obligation is to not let your assigned work here suffer."

The words of my father immediately resonated in my spirit: "Service is the rent that you pay for the space that you occupy here on earth."

My venue of service was the Tuskegee Federal Credit Union, where I advanced to the position of senior vice chairman of the board and coordinated a building program that enabled the institution to move into a new office building—debt-free. I became known as an unusual model of servant leadership during my life in that community that spanned nearly eighteen years. People would refer to me as "Mr. Community."

After I departed Tuskegee Institute to assume my long-held goal of serving as a chief financial officer (Morgan State University), I sat with the university president one evening. I asked him what had distinguished me from others that he had considered for the position of vice president for finance and management.

His response was, "Your record of service and leadership in the Tuskegee community made you stand out. We examined you very closely, and we were impressed with your leadership with the Tuskegee Federal Credit Union, the Tuskegee Housing Authority, the Tuskegee Industrial Development Authority, and the Tuskegee Model Cities Commission. We also noted your leadership role as an officer in the US Army Reserves."

Here was another affirmation of my father's early dictum regarding service. Later in life, I became familiar with the writings of Robert Greenleaf. His concept of servant leadership seemed to mirror the life that I had lived in Tuskegee and now in Baltimore, Maryland. These words of his stuck with me: "Servant leadership is a practical philosophy which support people who choose to serve first, and then lead in a way of expanding service to individuals and institutions. Servant leaders may or may not have formal positions. Servant leadership encourages collaboration, trust, foresight, listening, and the ethical uses of power and empowerment."

A final defining moment and then I will share some influences. In my first presidency at Schenectady County Community College, I sat in my office alone on the Sunday night before officially assuming my duties as president. There was no one in the building but the security official and me. As I sat on my sofa in a reflective mood, something seemed to come over me. It suddenly hit me that the future of that college—its students, faculty, and staff—was now in my hands. The status and reputation of the college in the community was in my hands. I was now about to assume an awesome responsibility. I would now have to put into practice everything that I had learned and cultivated over the years about servant leadership. As the late Paul Harvey would say, "You know the rest of the story," as I have now served as the president of three colleges and was asked to serve as the chancellor of the largest community college system in Texas.

Significant Influences

In his rousing sermons, Dwight L. Moody, the famous nineteenth-century evangelist, often told the moving story of a ship nearing the Cleveland Harbor during a violent storm on Lake Erie. The story supports the servant-leadership theme of this national conference and, hopefully, our individual quests to be models of servant leadership.

"On a dark and stormy night, when the waves rolled like mountains and not a star was to be seen, a boat, rocking and plunging, neared the Cleveland harbor . . .

'Are you sure this is Cleveland?' the captain asked, for he could only see the light from the lighthouse.

'Quite sure,' replied the pilot of the boat.

'But where are the lower lights, the lights along the shore to guide us?'

'Gone out, sir,' was the reply.

'Can we make the harbor?'

'Captain, we must make the harbor—otherwise, we perish, sir.'

With a strong hand and a brave heart, the old pilot turned the wheel. Alas, in the darkness, he missed the channel and, crashing upon the rocks, the boat was slivered and many a life lost in a watery grave."

The Reverend Mr. Moody would conclude his sermons with these words: "The Master will take care of the great lighthouse. Let us keep the lower lights burning."

I try to live by those words of the Reverend Mr. Moody. The story continues for there was one occasion when one of Mr. Moody's soloists, Philip P. Bliss, was so inspired that he wrote the words of music to the well-known hymn "Let the Lower Lights Be Burning." As this talk is about my life in abstract form, indulge me as I share the words of the hymn.

> Brightly beams our Father's mercy
> From His lighthouse evermore.
> But to us He gives the keeping,

Of the lights along the shore.
Let the lower lights be burning!
Send a gleam across the wave!
Some poor fainting, struggling seaman,
You may rescue, you may save.
Dark the night of sin has settled,
Loud the angry billows roar;
Eager eyes are watching, longing
For the lights along the shore
Trim your feeble lamp my brother!
Some poor sailor tempest tossed,
Trying now to make the harbor,
In the darkness may be lost.

I ask the question: Are you a lower light? You may be the only light in someone's darkness. So be the example of the Good Samaritan and heed the Master's own words in Matthew 5:16, "Let your light shine before men, that they may see your good deeds and praise your Father in heaven."

There is a second episode that comes from the work of one of the most popular and influential poets of the nineteenth century, Henry Wadsworth Longfellow. He was equally successful in lyric and narrative poetry, and he was a master of the sonnet. One of his most famous poems, "A Psalm of Life," speaks eloquently of life's purpose and reveals the moral impulse characteristic of the writings of Longfellow. He warns us that "time is fleeting" and gives us the striking metaphor which is characteristic of the writings of Longfellow. In the lilting words of that poem, the poet-preacher reminds us that life has a purpose beyond what we can see and that "the grave is not its goal." But the dominant note is optimistic action, inspired by great lives and a sense of destiny.

The Greeks inscribed the words "know thyself" above the temple of their oracle at Delphi. That dictum presents life's great quest. *Who am I? Why am I here? Where am I going? Whose am I?* Those are the quintessential questions if you would be the servant leader in the flat world that we live in.

You see, God has planted within us a relenting intuition to see beyond temporal horizons, and to press beyond the limits of the finite. A sense of destiny dominates us as servant leaders. Eternal forces ripple in our blood. Immortal cadences echo in our ears. Sublime visions flash upon the screen of our imagination. Eternity beckons as deep calls unto the depths that God has put in our souls. So the poet-preacher Longfellow challenges us as servant leaders to so live that "each tomorrow finds us farther than today."

Centuries before Longfellow, there was a certain traveler on the Jericho Road who came upon a man who had been beaten, robbed, disrobed, and left for dead in a ditch along the side of the road. Two other travelers had traversed along that same road, but dared not to stop and be of assistance. An unlikely traveler did stop and come to the aid of the fallen brother. He bound his wounds, put him on his beast, carried him to the next hamlet, left him in the care of a willing servant, left some money for his keep and care, and said if what he had left was not sufficient, on his return trip he would fully repay him.

My friends and fellow servant leaders, we live during times when we too are traveling along the contemporary Jericho Road. The contemporary Jericho Road has brothers and sisters whose conditions beckon to us as servant leaders to look beyond self and come to the aid of those in need.

The Challenge to Live Beyond Self

In Fosdick's 1920 book on *The Meaning of Service*, he uses the analogy from the Holy Land—rivers that run parallel to human life.

The Sea of Galilee and the Dead Sea are made of the same water. It flows down, clear and cool, from the mountain heights to the roots of the cedars of Lebanon. The Sea of Galilee makes beauty of it, for the Sea of Galilee has an outlet—it gets water to give. It gathers in its riches so that it may pour them out again to fertilize the Jordan plains.

But the Dead Sea, with the same water, makes a horror. For the Dead Sea has no outlet—it gets to keep. Notice this phrase of Khalil Gibran: "It is when you think less of yourself that you truly give."

I will not presume to tell you which direction you should go to live beyond self, but I would advise you, however, not to follow Yogi Berra's suggestion: "When you get to the fork in the road, take it." Rather, I would advise you to think of the words of Ralph Waldo Emerson, who challenges us when he advises, "Do not go where there the path may be. Go instead where there is no path, and leave a trail.

Albert Schweitzer was approached by a small cadre of individuals who thought they wanted to join him in Africa as missionaries. They asked him where were the roads, to which he replied, "If you are coming here looking for roads, don't come. I want people to come here and make roads."

I would add to that this thought—it is not the miles that you have traveled that count, it is the journey that you have yet to travel. We humans have shown ourselves capable of nobility, of kindness, and of generosity. We must draw our strength from those who exhibit the best that is in them. And let us remember, "To everything there is a season, and a time for every purpose under the heaven." And if this be not your season, it will come. Just keep planting seeds of service. For "service is the rent that you pay for the space that you occupy here on earth."

Understand one thing about the decisions we make on our journey. When we make a decision, it is just the beginning, and it will take us to places we had never dreamed of. If you listen to your heart, you will always make the right decision.

Think about this—we each have our own destiny. When we do not fulfill it, the soul of the universe is incomplete. To successfully make the journey and fulfill your destiny, you must always strive to be your best and always be prepared to not give up. It is important to continue on your journey in spite of the inevitable string of frustrations and missteps along the way. This is true because a journey through life is not without perils and defeats.

It is you who will determine the fate of the world that we pass on to our children and others. So never forget, everything you do has an impact not only on the organization that you work in, but also the world we live in. When you strive to always be better than you were, everyone around you also becomes better.

I conclude by saying that those who would lead in any walk of life should write their own stories in lives of service. Let those who would search for the nature of servant leadership look first for evidence of significant service. The more significant the service, the more likely the source will be rooted in simplicity. The simpler the source, the greater the leadership . . . May you always lead with your heart and the words of my father: "Service is the rent that you pay for the space that you occupy on earth. Always strive to live in a high-rent district."

RELATIONSHIPS ARE A MEASURE OF STEWARDSHIP

God has made each of us a steward or manager of the affairs of God on earth, and he has given us unique abilities and possessions for us to use in service. As stewards of God, our service should be rendered in the context of love and gratitude for the blessings bestowed on us.

Therefore, it is important that we do not become concerned with the amount that we have, but with the use of that which we have. Our life is perhaps the greatest of God's gifts, and it is this gift that carries the greatest responsibility—which is to use our minds in discovering God's plan in understanding ourselves and others. Our relationships with others and how they are managed represent a measure of our stewardship.

The stewardship of relationships operates at four levels—in the home, in the work setting, in social gatherings, and in the place of worship.

At home, we are responsible for religiously educating our children (if we are parents), and seeking the salvation of kindred. We should provide an environment for living and growing together as a family in love. Stewardship of relationships should recognize the fact that closeness brings conflicts, and that human nature tends to be disruptive. Therefore, the steward must be sensitive, loving, caring, and patient—compelled to take the risk of becoming a "wounded healer."

At work, the steward demonstrates both by precept and example— the ideal Christian behavior. This is a behavior involving risk and responsibility. We must risk opening and sharing ourselves to others— sharing our feelings, joys, and concerns. Likewise, we have the responsibility to listen, to be supportive, and to reaffirm our love and care for others. We are our brother's keeper. No man lives unto himself, for all men are social creatures living in a society of unity, yet diverse in a wide-ranging array of differences and uniqueness. Love respects the differences in others and allows them the right to express their unique heritage.

In social gatherings, our task as stewards is keenly akin to that in the work setting.

In the worship setting, believers are to be motivated for concerned effort living in partnership and unity as the family of God engaging in worship, celebration, and the crystallization of lasting friendships. This unity makes individual and group purposes possible.

The stewardship of relationships is indeed an awesome task—one that should not be taken lightly. The task is made difficult by the fact that the first step in the process of building relationships is personal: getting in touch with self, discovering also who we are and loving oneself. In learning to love oneself, we learn and discover how to truly love others. Building relationships is hard, but a worthy work that is required as stewards, and also as servant leaders.

As stewards of relationships, we must be persons with strong faith. I am reminded of this short item by an unknown author.

> Doubt sees the obstacles . . .
> Faith sees the way!
> Doubt seeks the darkest night . . .
> Faith sees the light.
> Doubt dreads to take a step . . .
> Faith soars on high.
> Doubt asks the question "Who believes?"
> Faith answers, "It is I."

This was an article in the Insights column of the *Dallas Morning News* when I served as the Interim Pastor of the St. John Missionary Baptist Church in Dallas.

THE ROLE OF PERSONAL LEADERSHIP

I n John Maxwell's book *The 21 Irrefutable Laws of Leadership*, he states that an individual's leadership ability determines their effectiveness. The lower an individual's ability to lead, the lower will be his or her effectiveness. Maxwell states that on a scale of 1–10, if your leadership ability is a 5, your leadership effectiveness will never be greater than a 4.

This law extends to teams and organizations as well. The effectiveness of an organization can never be greater than the personal leadership skills of the weakest link. If the leadership skills of the weakest link on a team are a 5, the effectiveness of the team can never be greater than a 4. It is important to recognize that everyone leads at some point in time. I am sure you all are familiar with the well-known analogy of the geese in flight. The same principle applies in our work—like the geese, everyone must be ready to step up and lead.

What Is Personal Leadership?

There are many definitions of the word *leadership*. Peter Drucker defined leadership as "lifting a person's vision to higher heights, raising a person's performance to a higher standard, and building a personality beyond its normal limitations." *Webster's* dictionary simply defines leadership as "the ability to lead." Both of those definitions handle certain aspects of the art. Yes, leadership is an art. Moreover, when done well, its beauty rivals the art of some of the world's masters.

At a Peter Lowe Success Seminar, the late General Norman Schwarzkopf said, "Leadership is the art, skill, talent, or ability to get others to do those things they do not normally or naturally want to do."

If his definition is extended, then personal leadership is the art, skill, talent, or ability to get YOU to do those things you do not normally or naturally want to do. *Personal leadership* means your ability to direct yourself to perform even when you do not necessarily want to.

The notable professional speaker Les Brown indicates that to get yourself to perform, sometimes "you just got to be hungry." Nothing develops hunger like purpose. Purpose is that thing that you were created to do. It is your life's mission. It is the one thing that helps you focus. Purpose will help you decide which projects you should propose and participate in, and which will just drain off your time. Purpose will get you going when fatigue has made a coward of you. In my opinion, purpose is the Holy Grail of performance, and it is at the very heart of the rewards and responsibilities accruing from a career in academic administration.

Let me share six steps with you that can provide the leadership needed and for which every organization is searching and seeking.

- *Develop the commitment to manifest greatness.* Recognize the simple fact that each of us has an intended level of greatness that extends into all areas of our lives. *Greatness*, in performance terms, is defined as "closing the gap between your actual level of performance and your potential for performance." So the first step is to develop the commitment to close the gap.
- *Change the things you think about all day long.* Ralph Waldo Emerson said, "We are what we think about all the day long." Most often, we maintain those thoughts, values, and beliefs that hold us back and deter our ability to manifest our intended greatness. There is a Scripture that I have an affinity for that says, "Be ye not conformed to the world, but be ye transformed by the renewing of your mind." That is the second step.
- *Discover and pursue your determined purpose.* Purpose gives you the kind of motivation that will wake you up early and keep you up late at night. It is the single most important factor of performance improvement at either the individual or the organizational level.
- *Find the energy between your calling and your vocation.* We each have a calling and a vocation. The calling is what we contribute to others, and our vocation is what we do to pay the bills while

we work in our calling. When we can develop synergy between the two, we find ourselves moving in the right direction all the time. There is no wasted effort. Your service work also moves you toward the accomplishment of professional goals.

· *Develop a plan.* Listen to this quote from a child: "If you plan on being great, you better develop a great plan." Most people spend more time planning their workdays and vacations than their lives. Our lives is the most important long-term project that we will ever manage.

· *Implement.* The final step is to implement or act according to your plan. You should engage in daily activities that move you closer to accomplishing the milestones that lead to the fulfillment of your determined purpose.

Achieving this may appear daunting, but it is quite simple. However, it does require a great deal of introspection. The great benefit is that in the end, you will finally know who you want to be when you "grow up," and the great manifestations of a lack of leadership ability will fade into the past.

LEADERSHIP IS ABOUT THE PEOPLE FOR WHOM WE ARE RESPONSIBLE

Servant leaders are described as collaborative, inclusive, engaging, and inspiring. Work groups in that setting are expected to be team-focused, democratic, matrixes, and participative. Everyone expects to have a voice.

In today's world, servant leaders need to develop and master what I describe as the three "A's." They are *agility*, *agency*, and *authenticity*. These attributes provide the foundation for success as a servant leader.

The first is agility. Agility, or the ability to lead nimbly in face of uncertainty, is the key to leadership success in today's ever-changing environment. Agility is more than the ability to act quickly, or to be responsive. It requires a strong sense of purpose that enables leaders to know what they stand for. Being rooted in a sense of purpose clarifies when to be open to change, when to stand one's ground, and how to act when faced with completely unknown territory. Agility is the fulcrum upon which servant leaders pivot.

The second is agency. Agency is the ability to make choices and enact them in your organization or work group. It means that rather than taking the path of least resistance, or being swept up in the dysfunctional routines, the servant leader determines for himself or herself what ought to be done and then does it. In a rapidly changing world where leaders have less and less bestowed authority, a strong sense of agency is critical.

The third "A" is authenticity. If agency is about accepting the responsibility to take action, authenticity is about doing so in ways that are consistent with the leader's own convictions and the challenges facing the organization. Authenticity is thus a double-sided obligation. It means being true to yourself and also to the people around you. In the context of the fact that a trust deficit exists for some leaders, authenticity matters more today than ever before.

Leaders of today must keep one foot in today and the other in the world of tomorrow. To accomplish that with some degree of effectiveness means that the servant leader must truly understand and embrace a certain imperative. Leadership is about the people for whom we are responsible. Disruption, change, and uncertainty demand stronger emotional connections between leaders and followers.

PART FOUR
THE PATH TO THE PRESIDENCY

If you can't be a tree on the top of the hill
Be a shrub in the valley, but be
The best little shrub on the side of the hill.
Be a bush if you can't be a tree.
—(Author Unknown)

Have You Heard the Call?
The Search Process
Five Reasons to Aspire to the Presidency
Stepping Through the Leadership Door as a College President
The Presidency as a Journey—Not a Destination
Anatomy of a New President
Essential Principles for New Presidents
Successful Presidents Court Risk and Change
Presidential Relationships: Build Them with Caution
Reflections after Three Decades of CEO Service
on the Business of Leading a College
The College President of the Future
"Emerging From Within"—How to Do It
Keys for Well-Rounded Leadership
The Leader's Covenant

HAVE YOU HEARD
THE CALL?

When it comes to careers, the most important bit of old-fashioned wisdom is that people are called to vocations like religion and the role of the pastor, engineering, science, law, education, the military, medicine—and leadership.

One needs to know if you are really called to leadership. If you are, acting on the call, leadership will benefit you, your family, and most of all, the people you lead. If you are not, you will be wasting your time, frustrating people, deluding yourself, and neglecting some other call that is your true path. So how can you know if you're called to leadership? Consider the following suggestions and observations based on my professional journey.

First, if all the benefits of leading were taken away from the job, would you still find yourself leading? Or would you still want to be in leadership? People who answer a call often say that they "can do no other." That phrase is attributed to Martin Luther, as a reason for opposing the religious authorities of his day, despite a high probability of a very bad outcome for him and his family. Whether he actually uttered the words or not, they capture the experience of one who is answering a call: "Here I stand, I can do no other."

Second, run through a worst-case scenario: Your efforts fail, no one follows, and you find yourself at a career rock bottom. What would you do? Most leaders would find another way to move forward. Some from the outside applaud their resilience, but that is not the internal experience. Leaders lead because they can do no other.

Third, see if your life matches a common profile. In leadership, people are drawn to the study of the field and examples of successful leaders. They love biographies of leaders in all parts of life, from heads of state to religious leaders to industrialists and corporate icons. Their minds wrestle with the patterns, and with the lack of patterns, as they work out their own leadership approach. The noted writer and educator Warren Bennis refers to leaders as "conceptualists"—they are drawn to the principles that make leadership function, as they also wrestle with how to apply them.

Look at the example of those who display early abilities. Steve Jobs and Bill Gates are two examples. Leadership prodigies were not necessarily out in front from the beginning, but they were refining their abilities; and some were only waiting for the right moment to step forward. Even in the quiet period, however, they were gaining respect—an awareness of themselves and their powers of influence.

Those called to leadership come to realize that they have a curiosity that they can't explain about the field of leadership, the people in it, and its true nature. This curiosity and natural abilities have always been with them.

As I reflect on leaders that caught my attention and whom I came to admire, I am reminded of a statement that the famed Dr. Louis Pasteur made to his medical students years ago. He would tell them, "Gentlemen, as you go through life, always take your life preserver. Your life preserver is curiosity."

Leaders find themselves unable to do anything else. People with this call can often spot others who have it. The greatest sin of people called to leadership is to confuse the reason we are doing it with the perks that come with the job.

In my case, I believe I am also called as a teacher. If there are those in any organization who find themselves with the leadership call, there is a lot you should be doing—even need to be doing. Read, reflect, and experiment. Notice your patterns. What do you find yourself doing? What aspects of leadership most appeal to you?

It is important to embrace the truism that leadership cannot be reduced to a formula or a set of steps. It is also a field with many charlatans, pretenders, and self-deluded people, most of them going for the goodies, rather than people who "can do no other."

All of the foregoing, as I tell my colleagues, is just "food for thought."

THE SEARCH PROCESS

The general rule is that, in order to reach the presidency, one should teach then get on the tenure track, become a department chair, and rise up the administrative ladder to serve as chief academic officer. That general rule does not apply today. While search committees come up with their list of experiences that they are seeking in a president, the expanding role of the college president and the impact of continuous change calls for a wider view of the profile needed in a new president.

You can look at all senior cabinet-level positions as leadership-in-training for the presidency today. It is all about being in a position that allows a person to get full exposure to both the internal and external skills and abilities that equip someone to be a strong candidate for a presidential opportunity.

Are higher education outsiders being hired for the top job? That is generally not the case, but it sometimes happens. This is a factor of search committees' wariness of people outside of the academy and the inability of these candidates to fully understand and appreciate the culture of a college environment.

Presidential searches have always had high stakes, but today's campus search committees and search firms have a more challenging task than ever before. Based on my experience in searching for presidents while chancellor of the seven-college Dallas County Community College District, these are points of note:

- Some promising candidates have concerns about confidentiality and opt not to go forward.
- Some view the process as too lengthy.
- In general, it takes a lot of work to get a highly successful person engaged in the process.

- The person a committee has an interest in may have to be cajoled to even look at the potential opportunity.
- It is not unusual for the initial pool to consist of 30–50 individuals.
- To some, the presidency is unappealing. They have seen the presidency up close and personal in their roles, so they have a pretty good sense of whether it is something that they want to be doing.
- The most popular reasons why some are not excited about getting into the process are: the time demands; the unappealing nature of the work; the incredible amount of energy, endurance, and capability to deal with a variety of constituencies; and the inclination to not want to leave a place where one is doing meaningful work—that is less challenging.
- Search firms, however, are encouraging boards and search committees to have an open mind.
- In the end, search firms and committees tend to gravitate to those candidates who will bring a stronger, deeper, firmer understanding of the academy.
- It is not a slam dunk, even for the most promising internal candidates. There is this two-edged sword. You have the benefit that everybody knows you, and you have the curse that everybody knows you.
- Just as search firms and candidates are searching for star candidates, they generally start with people from institutions who have held positions that would typically prepare them for president.
- There are some search committees with a firm view to only consider outside candidates.
- Search committees look carefully at candidates who not only have relevant experience in their profile, but also have undergone significant professional development experiences.

As higher education evolves, what it means to be a college president may well evolve. Clearly, the times are demanding institutions and senior executives to think creatively and differently about pedagogy, curricula, delivery systems, and the entire process. A close look at the expectations of presidents is in order. The nature of the job, the 24/7 aspect, means that it is heavy lifting in every direction. What I have provided are just thoughts for an aspiring candidate to ponder as they evaluate whether to aspire to the presidency.

FIVE REASONS TO ASPIRE TO THE PRESIDENCY

1. **A president's life is far from dull.**

   - It is a great job.
   - Stimulating and challenging.
   - Anyone who has a well-rounded personality and a strong profile would find the presidency exciting.

2. **The presidency is more than just a job.**

   - Presidents are obviously working hard to make things go well, but they are also absolutely devoted, absolutely committed, and absolutely gratified with the work that they are doing.

3. **It is a chance to make a real impact.**

   - People are drawn to the opportunity to make a difference.
   - To turn around a struggling college or to raise a stable institution to the next level.
   - To optimize the curriculum, or build new programs.
   - The strongest leaders are those who want to accomplish something, not just run something.

4. **The role is unique.**

   - The president is really the cross point between internal and external constituencies.

➢ People are really intrigued when they realize how they bridge those different worlds.

➢ The role is very appealing.

5. The journey there is eye-opening.

➢ Aspiring presidents must begin developing professional networks that will get you noticed, both at your present location and nationwide.

STEPPING THROUGH THE LEADERSHIP DOOR AS A COLLEGE PRESIDENT

I consider it a profound privilege and honor to have the opportunity to offer a few words of encouragement and inspiration to this remarkable leader that the college and community has chosen to provide leadership at perhaps the most challenging time in the history of the community college movement.

Let me begin my talk with a personal reference to establish context. My professional objective was to rise to the point of serving as the chief financial officer of a college or university. After seventeen-plus years of preparation, I reached what was for me the pinnacle of my career ambition and aspiration. I was elected the vice president for finance and management Morgan State University in Baltimore, Maryland.

Two years into that experience as a CFO, a friend and neighbor approached me and informed me that the president of the university where he was serving as a trustee had announced his plans to retire. He thought that I represented the profile of what they would be seeking. Not having even thought of being a college president, I was flattered, shocked, and humbled. After thanking him, I asked for some time to ponder the possibility. My first action was to call my mentor and seek his counsel. My mentor was the president of the institutions where I had served previously—Tuskegee Institute (now Tuskegee University). He was Dr. Luther H. Foster. He was my mentor because his preparation and career pattern was one that I tried diligently to emulate. He was trained as a business officer, obtained two graduate degrees, served in senior business officer roles at two institutions, and then ascended to the presidency.

Succinctly he shared the following with me: (1) warmest congratulatory words were offered, for it was not every day that one would be considered as having "presidential material"; (2) he then proceeded to tell me that the presidency was a "calling," and I needed to be confident that I was truly called to that level of service; and (3) was I comfortable in the belief that I was in a position to "lead leaders," many of whom would be more expert than me in their areas of specialty. He talked further about the life of a president, the family situation, the demands, and also the rewards.

After pondering those points that he offered to me, I elected to not have my name placed in nomination. It was two and a half years later before that I was indeed "called," and that I was now prepared to "lead leaders." I applied for the presidency of Schenectady County Community College in Upstate New York, and I did what many considered the unthinkable at that time. That a college CFO would be named a college president, and that the CFO would be successful in his first attempt to ascend to the presidency.

As I matured as a college president and moved to two other presidencies, I resolved that a part of my calling was to prepare others to assume the daunting task of preparing to become a college president. Thirteen of my former colleagues have ascended to this august level. Your president is number 13, and like a parent, she is my youngest child and a favorite.

From the first time that I met a somewhat wild-eyed young lady desperately looking for the president of El Centro College at the Dallas Love Field, I have taken her under my wings and did all that I felt necessary to mold, shape, and prepare her for this position that she now proudly holds. Like her mentor, she too was successful in the first presidency that she pursued. And, I might add, she is a president at a college that is clearly not a run-of-the-mill institution. To the trustees and the larger community, you are to be commended for selecting her. I thank you. Although she is in that crucial first one-hundred days, I am confident that you will grow to appreciate her vision, style, leadership qualities, and her abundant human qualities.

She is what Jim Collins, the author of *Good to Great*, would call a "level-5 leader." Let me briefly describe the level-5 leader. This is an individual who blends extreme personal humility with intense professional will and skill. Leaders who possess this paradoxical combination of traits are catalysts for the statistically rare event of transforming a good college into a great institution.

Such leaders are a study in duality. They are modest and willful, shy and fearless. Level-5 leadership is not the only requirement for transforming a good college into a great institution, but it is essential. Good-to-great transformation just does not happen without such a leader at the helm.

Level-5 leaders pursue what I call the three "D's"—disciplined people, disciplined thought, and disciplined action. Leading is tough work. Leading well is even more difficult under the challenges and circumstances facing community colleges today. Yesterday's methods and mind-sets are insufficient. The rapid rate of change as we move deeper into the twenty-first century has created a need for those who would at a higher dimension than what we see today.

Mere mental or physical manipulation is not sufficient. Organizations and societies have evolved beyond traditional modes of influence. People want more. Stakeholders want more. The effective leader of today's world is intentional in creating a synergy for change and organizational vitality.

As we move deeper into the twenty-first century, American higher education confronts multiple issues: access, accountability, student success, cost, productivity, diversity, and something that is emerging rapidly called "performance-based" funding. In my view, what is perhaps above all these issues to the public argument over the mission and purpose of higher education, and whether it is to be viewed as a public benefit or a personal benefit?

Our colleges and universities are asked to serve many gods. The god of economic utility—get a job and be competent; the god of consumerism—spend money and acquire material possessions; the god of multiculturalism—to accept and respect differences—just to name three such gods. The question can be asked: are those adequate gods? I would say there is an additional "god." That is, we should be committed to launching all who enter and exit our portals on a search for life's meaning.

What might the future of higher education look like? Will market pressures distort the search for truth? Will faculty become hired hands and entrepreneurs rather than discoverers of truth and mentors of human potential? Will college presidents become captains of enterprise, the new CEOs, rather than leaders of learning and service? Will the house of intellect become a house of merchandisers where faculty are salespeople, hawking their wares to credential-hungry students?

What, then, is a college for? It is the home of our hope. It is the conservator of the record of our nobility and our barbaric tendencies and practices. It is the theater of our artistic impulses. It is a forum where dissent over purpose and performance may be seen as evidence that higher education is meeting its responsibilities.

It is a place where all—students, faculty, staff—are called to ask what it is that brings meaning to their lives and makes them glad to be alive and able to be "of service." It is, above all, a place where the humanizing force of our curiosity and wonder is celebrated. A place that is critical of conventional wisdom. It is a place that is hospitable to controversy. It is a place for the dreamers of the day.

Madam President, it is our duty to dream—to imagine what the world could be, and what it should be. Such dreaming is no idle pursuit. Quite the contrary, it is what defines us as human. It could well be the reason we exist. For without a dream, we are limited and lessened. Bound to the solitary confinement of what is, or was. As humans, and as leaders, we must embrace what might be. We dream because the dream is what makes tomorrow better. And yet no mere dream can make tomorrow better. The dream is necessary, but singly, it is insufficient. It is a vital step, but just the first step. It is the rung we stand on to see the space beyond.

Go forth and serve boldly as the president of this wonderful institution that you now lead. You are well-prepared; use your lessons learned well. This was the address delivered by the author at the inauguration of Dr. Toni Pendergrass.

THE PRESIDENCY AS A JOURNEY: NOT A DESTINATION

- ➤ Serendipity does play a factor.
- ➤ It is common for aspiring presidents to endure five to ten searches before securing a position as president.
- ➤ Give little credence to conventional wisdom regarding the type of institution.
- ➤ Problems that presidents encounter differ only by degree. No college or university president is free of these challenges, and no "good fit" is going to silence them.
- ➤ Do not be intimidated by the extra hurdles that women and minorities may face.
- ➤ The climb is rigorous.
- ➤ The work is time-consuming, tiring, and sometimes frustrating; but we can exert some control over time.
- ➤ The diversity of days can be exhilarating.
- ➤ You must be willing to take leaps of faith; be ready to step off the cliff every day.
- ➤ Balance all the risks and demands with the eclectic, the excitement, and even the power, for this position gives one the opportunity to serve the greater goals of our civilization.
- ➤ Our lives as presidents, and the journeys that led us here, are not terror attacks. In fact, they are by and large, hugely rewarding—if we can allay the hubris that makes us think we can always plan it all. I keep this thought clearly in focus: "It is good to have an end to the journey forward, but it is the journey that matters, in the end."

➢ Remember the words of Agatha Christie: "Is there any particular spot where one can put one's finger and say that it all began that day, at such a time, and such a place, with such an incident—the answer is no."

THE ANATOMY OF A NEW PRESIDENT

➤ Great communicator: Must deliver a consistent message to a growing web of constituents.

➤ Humble by necessity: Realizes the cult of personality is kaput; focuses attention on the organization rather than himself/herself.

➤ Technophile: Keeps in constant touch via technology gadgets, gizmos, and groups.

➤ Accountable to governing board: Understands the best way to avoid and run it is to share information with the board. Practice the "no-surprise" principle.

➤ Team builder and hierarchy buster: Recognizes the value of eliminating layers and bureaucracy where necessary; prefers team building to star-building.

➤ Actor.

➤ Judge.

➤ Visionary.

➤ Leader.

➤ Mind reader.

➤ Problem solver.

➤ Psychologist.

➤ Coach.

➤ Strategist.

ESSENTIAL PRINCIPLES FOR NEW PRESIDENTS

- ➤ A commitment to excellence.
- ➤ Lead from a personal vision, mission, and set of values.
- ➤ Develop a passion for the work of a president.
- ➤ Lead for results.
- ➤ Be honest.
- ➤ Be fair and respectful.
- ➤ Be humble.
- ➤ Be adaptable.
- ➤ Know your business.
- ➤ Delegate, but monitor.
- ➤ Do sweat the small stuff.
- ➤ Accept criticism, share the glory.
- ➤ Building trusting relationships.
- ➤ Treat people differently, based on their strengths.
- ➤ Set high standards, but give people the freedom and responsibility to do their jobs.
- ➤ Performance reviews must be honest, exacting, and an integral part of the job.
- ➤ People learn most when teaching others.
- ➤ Effective leaders earn respect, but do not have to be liked.

SUCCESSFUL PRESIDENTS COURT RISK AND CHANGE

College and university leaders often avoid risk, viewing it as potentially controversial at best—and at worst, a prelude to a possible failure. Yet, as countless contemporary examples demonstrate, "playing it safe" no longer works in higher education because, while some colleges are basking in past accomplishments, others are gaining a competitive edge.

To thrive in a world in which rapid change is the only constant, effective institutions today must be models of innovation, openness, and competitiveness. Effective leaders must take calculated risks to move their organizations ahead. If a college or a university is not where it should be, a new marketplace must be created. Continuous reinvention is the key to dynamic leadership, both long- and short-term survival.

I offer these hallmarks of leaders who are willing and able to successfully harness change for the aspiring, new, and also seasoned presidents.

Be proactive. When pursuing new ventures and opportunities, it is usually better to be first than to be the best. The academy is known for its deliberate decision-making processes, which often delay pivotal decisions until the window of opportunity has closed. Successful leaders/presidents act decisively to seize the moment at hand.

Find a need and fill it. The most basic definition of marketing is to look for synergistic partnership opportunities.

Look for win-win opportunities. This is the area in which the president must be an innovative risk-taker and exploit the wisdom of his team members.

Minimize the risk. Being a catalyst for change does not mean acting with disregard for the consequences of failure. Avoid the shortcoming

121

of this kind of thinking—"if we build it, or put it together, people will come."

Seek the "silver lining" in the cloud. Necessity is frequently the mother of invention, and success is often born in the wake of failure and tragedy. But there is frequently a nugget that can be mined even from undesirable events, if we look hard enough.

As stressful as organizational change may be, the alternatives—stagnation, decline, and eventual death—are even less palatable. Successful leaders/presidents seek, welcome, embrace, and manage risk to move their institutions ahead.

PRESIDENTIAL RELATIONSHIPS: BUILD THEM WITH CAUTION

N avigating a new presidency is a lot like piloting a ship through a narrow channel. Oftentimes, the surface appears calm, but sandbars and jagged rocks lurk just below the surface waters. During my tenure, I have seen similar situations time and time again with promising new presidencies whose ships never dock because of early fatal mistakes.

All these presidents had begun their presidencies with great potential. They had met or exceeded performance benchmarks—increased enrollment, student recruitment and retention increases, stemmed the flow of red ink—but still failed. What went wrong?

In many of the cases of failure, rocky relationships with key constituencies sink more promising presidencies than any other single factor. While competent performance is a given, it must be accompanied by equally solid relationships. Failure to heed early warning signs can portend a shipwreck ahead. Several factors feed this common scenario.

The "fix it" scenario. Especially in turnaround situations, expectations that you will come in and immediately deliver a "quick fit" abound. Everyone will offer you advice, most of it well-intended and some of it sound, but short-term solutions to long-term challenges will not result in a long-term relationship.

The overreaction scenario. You may have been hired in response to a specific campus need or issue, or perhaps the search committee was seeking a leader similar to or as different as possible from your predecessor. Either way, you must avoid the temptation to act quickly and decisively, and wrongly. Beware of draconian change in response to pressure from well-meaning campus constituencies.

The expectations scenario. New presidents frequently comment that they came to the presidency from a specialized area and did not fully realize its comprehensive nature until they had actually assumed the office. Even before the boxes in your new office are completely unpacked, various constituencies will likely beset you, each with its own unspoken needs and agendas.

It is tempting to build popularity by responding immediately to "squeaky wheels." Take your time before making promises you may not be able to keep. Most leaders who try to be all things to all people tend to fail both. Here is some time-proven guidance that has worked for virtually every effective transformational leader (most new presidents today are expected to be transformers).

Run from day 1. One of our most visionary presidents, Theodore Roosevelt, said, "In the time for a decision, the best thing to do is the right thing. The worst thing to do is nothing."

Take calculated risks. Effective leaders must take calculated risks to move the institution ahead. If your institution is stagnant, it is in decline. If you are not where you want to be in the marketplace, you may need to create a whole new marketplace. Continuous reinvention is the key to dynamic leadership.

Communicate a passionate vision. Your highest priority is to develop and communicate an overriding plan to guide your actions. Without a passionate vision, your presidency risks gradually deteriorating into a mindless set of ad hoc adjustments to emerging circumstances. Avoid falling into the trap of managing from crisis to crisis, exhausting resources, staff, and yourself in the bargain.

Do not try to go it alone. Hire the best people that you can find, support them, delegate, and avoid micromanaging. Motivating leaders are secure enough to hire, retain, and promote men and women of accomplishment who know more than they do in their specific areas of expertise. Share credit for success, accept accountability for failure, be visible on campus, and keep appropriate social distance; too much informal interaction can reduce your effectiveness. The college presidency can be a lonely profession, but don't look for friendships among your key constituents.

While none of these suggestions will ensure a safe and secure mooring, following them will go a long way toward helping you make the crucial leap from the "honeymoon" to a successful and happy long-term institutional marriage.

REFLECTIONS AFTER THREE DECADES OF CEO SERVICE ON THE BUSINESS OF LEADING A COLLEGE

I n 1980, I realized what a college or university administrator would consider the epitome or capstone in his career pattern—reaching the level of college president. This was realized when I moved to the presidency of Schenectady County Community College of the State University of New York System, following two decades of service as a university business officer. Four and a half years earlier, when I had been appointed a vice president of finance and management at Morgan State University, I had realized what my ultimate career goal was then. For the purpose of this article, it should be noted that when appointed as president of that institution, I was the first African-American president in the SUNY System.

Throughout my tenure as a college president in three different settings, to my role as system chancellor, I have extolled the imperative of viewing the educational enterprise in the context of a business. The purpose of this paper is to expand on the business approach and to share my outlook with other interested parties.

The Business Approached Defined

The idea of leading a college as a business is more than a simile, or figure of speech. It is a mind-set that focuses on service quality and customer satisfaction measured long-term. An effective college must provide a service that fills the needs of its students, former students, and graduates throughout their lives. Consider this analogy of a person who buys an automobile at age twenty-one that would serve him for fifty years! Let's turn the analogy around and make the point differently, still using the automobile as the focal point.

An automobile dealer is more interested in serving the customer than in selling the car. There is one dealer in Dallas who has this mantra: "We will seek to have customers for life." If a dealership serves a customer well, it increases the chances of having a repeat customer who buys more than one car, has that car serviced in that dealership, and tells his friends. If all goes well, the customer's children and grandchildren will buy their cars at the same dealership.

Since the measure of an effective graduate of an institution may take ten to thirty years to assess, faculty and staff must focus on the quality of the service provided, within the demands of the educational marketplace.

My concept of the college incorporates two views. First as a service provider, and second as a self-rejuvenating nonprofit corporation. The two features are connected. As a service provider, the institution has two goals. The first is to develop, retain, and teach the knowledge that is central to American culture and history, and to a growing global marketplace.

Second, the institution must provide opportunities for students to cooperate, compete, follow, lead, listen, speak, develop friendships, and become aware of the role required of an educated person in society. If these two goals are met, a student should find an area of interest that leads to career development. If all of the foregoing is to work—that is, if the college is going to able to executive its mission, it must be a financially viable enterprise.

From a president's perspective, the business of leading a college is making sure that resources are available and used effectively in the right academic and service areas, by the right people, to ensure that high-quality service is always rendered. This means that it is essential that the right people are in place to deliver academic and educational support services to students, while a part of the president's time is devoted to resource development in the broadest possible context.

Key Factors in a Business Approach to College Leadership

➢ Develop a systems awareness of the institution.
➢ Focus on mission management. A leader must have the ability to see both forest and individual trees. Central to focus is always mission. Mission management means that all decisions are made within the context of a clearly articulated mission statement.
➢ Board governance. The board must govern from the standpoint of the financial viability of the institution. For without this awareness, the board loses its authority and its power. The CEO must see this task as a primary one.
➢ The working relationship of board chair and president. The relationship that must develop is that of a partnership based on trust. The board chair and the president must share a systemic understanding of the interrelatedness of the various parts of the institution. They must be in agreement that the president will manage the mission of the college and that the board will hold the president accountable for that management. Finally, to ensure that the board understands their fiduciary responsibilities.
➢ Operations and fiscal management.
➢ Staff training.
➢ The customer as a stakeholder.
➢ The products. It is the responsibility of the faculty and staff to create the finest teaching/learning experience possible for students. What we sell is both the trees and the forest. The trees are the classes, laboratories, instructional services, and practicum that comprise educational pedagogy. There are also trees in another part of the forest. These are the full range of out-of-class activities, to include community-learning experiences, clubs and organizations, and other organized activities. The combination of these two groves of trees makes up the college forest, which is an ecosystem that is more than the sum of the parts.

Operating the college as a business means taking seriously all the tools and techniques available to accomplish the institutional mission. The microscope and telescope must be used interchangeably in this process. The telescope consists of systemic views, outcomes, and training, the relationship to the board and president, and strategic planning.

The microscope is for mission, management, customers, operations, fiscal management, and governance. George Keller, in his book *Academic Strategy*, made this point well: "What is needed is a rebirth of academic improvement . . . one that combines educational policy and planning with financial administration, one that shows passionate concern for the long-term health of America's best colleges, one that has an agreed-upon strategy for the institution's role and objectives for action."

The college as we know it now will continue to change substantially. There will be an entrepreneurial explosion. Presidents—and those desiring to rise to that level, who understand the business of operating an institution—will be prepared. They will embrace the reality that a president plays interpersonal, informational, and decisional roles. In discharging the interpersonal roles, the president must be a figurehead, leader, and liaison. In discharging the informational roles, the president must be a monitor, disseminator, and spokesperson. In discharging the decisional roles, the president must be an entrepreneur, disturbance handler, resource allocator, and negotiator.

What an exciting challenge awaits those who are not fainthearted.

THE COLLEGE PRESIDENT OF THE FUTURE REFLECTIONS OF A FOUNDER

A small group of African-American college presidents who had broken the color barrier and advanced to become college presidents, without any specialized training, other than holding a doctoral degree, and now serving in a senior administrator role, decided that we should aid other aspirants by crafting a unique professional development program for that purpose. We founded the President's Round Table for that purpose. I played a key role in the establishment of the organization based on my prior experience in preparing individuals to strive to become chief financial officers.

The founding group assembled in Pittsburgh in mid-2014, and each of us provided "reflections." My reflections are abstracted and provided here for other aspiring presidents to consider.

Those college leaders who take advantage of external change will thrive; those who do not could go over the proverbial cliff quickly. "Adapt to changes through innovation and change, or die" is the single most important characteristic of any college CEO who wants to succeed. You ask the question—"Why is the ability to capitalize on external change so important?" It is important because external change is more frequent, more volatile, and more uncertain than ever. External forces are the drivers behind the student success/completion mandate that we are all addressing today.

This is not to say that the time-honored attributes of CEOs are not relevant. They are as important as ever, but the CEO of the future has to learn new skills and exercise his or her judgment accordingly. The traditional attributes of a CEO—character, integrity, vision, team-building, inspiring others, and communication—have been bundled, packaged, and repackaged. They are known, and they are being practiced; but in today's environment (to use a term from the game of poker), they are merely the table stakes. The CEO of today and the future must adapt and take advantage of the external changes that are unstoppable. They include the following.

Adapt to a fast-paced and uncertain world. In years past, we could count on stability—if not all the time, certainly for long stretches of time. Those days are in the past. Today, volatility is the norm rather than the exception, and that shows no signs of reverting to the days of yesteryear. The leader of the future will have to be extremely nimble and agile in order to adapt quickly to change.

The personal computer was once the defining technology across all industries. Today it has declined rapidly in comparison to mobile devices, phones, and the cloud computing that enables those devices to behave as the personal computers of the past. We see evidence today that, for the most part, by the time we have figured out a strategy for making optimal use of a device, that instrument is out-of-date.

Address the talent shortage. Across all industries, real talent remains scarce—particularly the expertise to develop the systems and the teams to capitalize on the changes on the horizon and beyond. It is believed that sometimes we focus too much on leadership development and not enough on knowledge and expertise. Leaders of the future need to find such people and figure out how to attract them. Rather than searching for so-called born leaders, if any do exist, CEOs and their teams need to find experts with leadership potential and then coach and develop them.

Just as at any other time, the CEOs of the future will need to be multitalented, multifaceted, personable visionaries who can recognize opportunity and seize it. Future leaders need to be able to adapt to the volatile external forces, those things they cannot see, and to create opportunity where others see none.

Thriving in the face of unstoppable trends requires the leader of the future to cultivate these capabilities:

- The ability to detect the external changes that matter despite their complexity and uncertainty.

- Being psychologically prepared to change course, even if it means shifting away from core competencies or key people.
- Being prepared to move fast in unfamiliar and perhaps low-margin growth markets and to shift decision-making to local contexts.
- Being focused on turning experts into leaders rather than leaders into experts.

Understand the importance of being a servant leader. The CEO of the future must understand that leadership is not about those of us in senior executive positions. It is not about perks, our feelings, our ego, or even our span of control. Leadership is about the people for whom we are responsible. Along with the title of chief executive officer comes a heavy load.

Servant leaders are described as collaborative, inclusive, engaging, and inspiring. Work groups in such settings are expected to be team-focused, democratic, matrixed, and participative; for everyone expects to have a voice.

In today's world, servant leaders need to develop and master what I describe as the three essential "A's" of *agility, agency,* and *authenticity.* Those attributes provide the foundation for the CEO of the future to realize success as a servant leader.

Leaders of today and the CEO of the future must keep one foot in today, and the other in the world of tomorrow. To accomplish this with some degree of effectiveness means that the servant leader must truly understand and embrace the imperative that leadership is about the people for whom we are responsible. Disruption, change, and uncertainty demand stronger emotional connections between leaders and followers.

EMERGING FROM WITHIN—HOW TO DO IT

residents who are promoted to the top spot from within must transform their relationships with former peers who are now subordinates. They must also balance the needs of the entire institution and not show any partiality toward the college/area that he/she formerly headed. The leadership challenge takes on even greater significance when the new CEO inherits a team already in place.

How you assemble a team is critical to your success. Based on my experience, I have crafted eight fundamental principles that could be helpful for consideration.

➢ Clarify your mandate.
➢ Leverage time by focusing on distinct types of learning.
➢ Identify critical alliances.
➢ Get the right team in place through modifications.
➢ Lay the groundwork for effective communication.
➢ Secure early wins.
➢ Shape your vision.
➢ Build and use a balanced advice network.

I will expand on getting the right team in place and laying the groundwork for effective communication.

Getting the Right Team in Place

➢ These are key questions to ask the team:

- Have they remained current on technologies, trends, and methods?
- Are they a positive influence in the institution?
- Do they care only about what is best for their assigned area, or can they balance that with what is essential for the entire institution?
- Do they know how to cooperate, and have they been expected to do that in the past?
- Do they work well as a team in the normal course of events, or only when there is a crisis?
- How is this group perceived by the layer of managers under them? Are they respected or feared?
- Do they complement one another? Does the collection of abilities they have complement yours?
- Are there other individuals who should be on the senior management group, but are not? If so, why?

➢ Provide basic guidelines on acceptable and unacceptable proposals.
➢ Give negative feedback quickly and gently.
➢ Observe and assess your inherited team in these areas:

- Competence
- Judgment
- Energy
- Focus
- Relationships
- Trust

➢ With the knowledge gained, restructure your team as necessary.

- Keep in place.
- Keep and develop.
- Move to another position.
- Observe for a needed period of time.

- Replace (low priority)
- Replace (high priority)

➤ Once your team is in place, apply the elements of great staff management that one has studied and learned will directly impact your success.

- Clear expectations.
- Materials, equipment to perform tasks.
- Opportunity to do their best daily.
- Receive recognition.
- Supervisor cares.
- Development encouraged.
- Opinion seems to count.
- Institutional mission makes the job seem important.
- Fellow employees committed to quality work.
- Make the work your best friend.
- Receive information about performance progress.
- Provide development opportunities.

Lay the Groundwork for Effective Communication

➤ Adjust or create a new formal communication system.
➤ Utilize or create an informal grapevine vehicle that is trustworthy.
➤ Use both of the above to tap into what is on the minds of the employees whose beliefs and feelings are most important.
➤ Motivate the team to understand, align with, and commit to your business strategy.
➤ Work on managing information overload.
➤ Involve key people in critical information flows.
➤ Pay attention to team members not on the same page—inconsistent messages.
➤ Work on leader visibility.
➤ Pay attention to team members not understanding their role and/or do not have the skills needed to carry out that role.
➤ As the leader, set the tone for ethical conduct.

KEYS FOR WELL-ROUNDED LEADERSHIP

E ffective leadership is not a single skill. It has many distinct dimensions that come to the forefront in different situations throughout a career. What follows are suggested areas that leaders should pay attention to in order to develop and grow as a leader, along with a small sampling of what I call "leadership quips" as memory joggers.

Directional leadership. The most obvious leadership dimension focuses on strategic issues. Where are you going? What direction is your institution and workforce headed in? How will you get to where you want to go? Remember that this dimension includes both "hard" and "soft" leadership skills.

Interpersonal influence. This area addresses your relationships with the wide variety of institutional stakeholders—internal and external. Pay special attention to your skills in coaching, mentoring, managing performance, and communicating.

Personal knowledge. How well do you know yourself? Your motivations? Your weaknesses? Your attitude, behavior, values, and actions tell people everything they need to know about your competence as a leader. Look for every opportunity to develop your honesty and self-discipline fully.

Implementation skills. This is the hands-on application of your responsibilities. Your technical and operational knowledge are crucial. How well do you follow through on decisions? Do you know how to overcome roadblocks and obstacles? How well do you influence other people to get things done? Do you stay on top of industry trends? Do you strengthen relationships with the team members around you as you execute plans and assignments?

Leadership Quips and Memory Joggers

- It only takes a spark. Enthusiasm is that kindling spark which marks the difference between leaders in every activity and the laggards who put in just enough to get by.
- An executive is the man or woman who decides; sometimes he/she decides right, but always he/she decides.
- An army of deer led by a lion is more to be feared than an army of lions led by a deer.
- Communication is the key to being an effective leader.
- The executive exists to make sensible exceptions to general rules.
- The essence of real leadership is to allow your team members to see your need and desire for learning. Your actions speak more than your words. Today's leaders must be students of change first, before they become teachers of change to others.
- When you join your organization, you will find there is a willing body of team members who ask from you nothing more than the qualities that will command their respect, their loyalty, and their commitment. They are perfectly ready and eager to follow you so long as you can convince them that you have those qualities. When the time comes that they are satisfied that you do not possess them—your future is dim, if not lost. Your usefulness as a leader becomes suspect.

THE LEADER'S COVENANT

The effective leader serves four masters: the institution, the team as a whole, the team's individual members, and the organizational mission.

What will inspire your team to follow your lead? How do you win their trust and get them to believe in you and your mission? You simply ask, "What's in it for them?" And then you give it to them.

What follows are ten behaviors that describe a leader any team member would love and choose to follow. If you can embrace these behaviors honestly, communicate them to your team, and demonstrate them daily in your team interactions, you will definitely get your team's attention, respect, and enthusiasm for the goal. This is what the team members want to hear from me, and they constitute the Leader's Covenant. I suggest this covenant to emerging, new, and experienced leaders.

> ➤ I will lead this team. I will not facilitate it, manage it, employ fuzzy collaborative management techniques, waffle, fake it, play games, obfuscate, obscure, abandon, forsake, desert, relinquish, abdicate, or in any other way undermine the pure leadership role you have the right to expect from me. In executing this role, I will provide direction, guidance, support, organization, initiative, and courage.
>
> ➤ I will provide you with a mission statement and clarify it as needed to achieve full team understanding of our goal.
>
> ➤ To achieve this mission, I pledge you my energy, my intelligence, my empathy, and my commitment. My personal goal is to earn and maintain your respect, spark your enthusiasm, and inspire your creative energy as we work together on this mission.

> ➢ I will provide you with a document identifying the initial structure of this team. It will include members' names and contact information, identification and definition for all individual roles, and clear expectations of what those roles require in terms of responsibility and accountability. This document will serve as a starting point for our discussion of team structure.

> ➢ I will acknowledge and respect the team's importance and role in achieving a successful result and will consult you prior to making any institutional commitments that would alter our mission.

> ➢ I will communicate all matters of importance to the team and/or to individual team members fully and in a timely manner, using whatever communication system the team deems appropriate.

> ➢ I will engage with you and involve you as we work with our clients to solve problems, come to decisions, and ultimately achieve our mission.

> ➢ I will be open to and actively seek individual suggestions for improving the team's process, the work to be done, and the final deliverables.

> ➢ I will respond immediately to team concerns and actively work to remove barriers to team progress.

> ➢ I will respond immediately to any concerns you may have about my leadership behaviors as expressed in this covenant. If, at any time, you feel that I am not living up to my commitments to the team, I expect you to bring it to my attention before it gets in the way of our success.

My covenant is completed with this final statement: "I look forward to being a part of this team and am excited about the work we will be doing together. I hope you feel the same way. I also hope that you can utilize this covenant in your individual team-building activities."

PART FIVE

END NOTES

SOME SAY—YOU DO

Don't we all wonder at the
Work that is done
In our behalf on the run . . . .
Seemingly ceaseless
Admired by all
But who among us makes the call
To say "thank you."

We each feel you know
How grateful we are,
How your standards of
Excellence are expected,
For you all ways do more than is prescribed to do,
No challenge is rejected.

When accolades should be the fare,
You receive a pat on the back
You've done it again—
What's new?
We think more than we say
"Thank you."

On reflection, this mighty display of effort
Achieved by a man with a permanent smile,
Is powered by goals and a love for people . . .
Rank and file.

If aware of effort expended,
We each would shout anew.
We don't really take for granted
All the wonderful things you do.

THANK YOU!

—Pattie Powell, DCCCD Trustee Emeritus (2010)

CONCLUDING PERSONAL REFLECTIONS ON LEADERSHIP

My view is that successful leadership is more of an art where the basics—competency, knowledge, management, proficiency, interpersonal skills, wisdom, vision, goals and priority setting—are important first conditions. But there is a second factor—the unique creativity of the artist or leader in the use of the basics, which can produce success.

Techniques differ, as do the situations where leadership artistry is employed; hence there is no single template. All that can be offered by an experienced leader is some personal reflections on what seems to have worked for him. That has been the thrust and focus of this book.

As I have been a leader in a number of settings outside of the academic sector, I thought it might be interesting in this final essay to reflect my personal findings on leadership that I believe have been useful for me in diverse settings. I have selected five out of the array of lessons learned and reflected in the parts of this book, as highlights. Underlying all of them is the basic given that to be a successful leader, you must be willing to listen and learn from your experiences all along the way. Always keep in focus that to be a successful leader, one must be a leadership lifetime learner.

- Rely upon trust, individual talent, and initiative.
- Treasure and protect a reputation for honesty and integrity.
- Value collective wisdom and team effort.
- Nurture future talent and plan succession.
- Avoid the dangers of the "power syndrome" and appreciate the value of dissent.

Rely Upon and Trust Individual Talent and Initiatives

The best leader understands the power of unleashing individual talent by offering persons the opportunity to be enterprising and to make a contribution. From my first leadership job, I learned the value of the opportunity to see leadership at the top that I would subsequently try to offer other young men and women later in life when I had the opportunity.

Treasure and Protect a Reputation for Honesty and Integrity

In my opinion, the greatest asset of successful leaders is their reputation for honesty and integrity. They are consequently perceived as a person whom "followers" can trust—a person in whom people will have faith.

Value Collective Wisdom and Team Effort

A frequent failing of some in leadership roles is the self-image of omnipotence and infallibility. Because you are the leader, you believe that—by definition—you have ultimate wisdom. I have found that very few leaders have a monopoly on wisdom. And, although the best leaders have a higher capacity for making good decisions, they also recognize that their decisions are strengthened and implementation is improved by relying upon the collective wisdom of their colleagues and subordinates.

Nurture Future Talent and Plan Succession

One of the greatest derelictions of leaders is their failure to prepare or nurture their successors. I have often wondered whether this neglect is due to the ego-dominant personalities of certain leaders, which will not tolerate those individuals who might have precisely the independence that would make them leaders.

Succession planning—preparing for your CEO successor—is vitally important, but there is another dimension that is even more neglected.

That is the nurture of non-CEO leaders, the second and third tier who are so vital to the success of the institution. They are also leaders and should not be overlooked. I trust that the reader will have seen the emphasis that I have placed on this topic in other essays contained here.

Avoid the Dangers of the Power Syndrome—Appreciate Dissent

Over the years, I have learned two important dangers of leadership and governance in any setting: how to exercise power and how to avoid its corruptive influence.

The starting point lies in how a leader deals with power. The greatest danger in possessing power is that it frequently produces a dramatic transformation in a leader's attitudes and behavior.

Power all too often becomes a narcotic that feeds on itself and contains hostile viruses that can reduce a leader's effectiveness. I have repeatedly observed the ease with which being in a position of power corrupts, causing a leader to become arrogant and dictatorial. Soon that type of leader is convinced that they are solely responsible for all the successes, while it is others or those beneath the leader who were the ones who were inadequate that caused the failures. Imperiousness, in turn, easily produces insulation from critical or divergent views and impedes the channels of communication. Worst of all is the leader's transformation into a papal-like absolute infallibility.

The second dimension of power corruption is the compulsive tendency to produce change. The new leader feels a compelling urge to achieve an immediate imprint as a symbol of his or her era. Over the years, I have never ceased to be amazed at those selected to lead who fell into the trap of trying to force through their own vision and concept for the future, too often for the sake of change alone.

An important counterbalance to the "power syndrome" is a leader's willingness to encourage and welcome honest criticism and contrarian views. I have had one or two immediate direct reports who are willing to disagree with me or to criticize me openly (but privately) because they know I want to hear their honest opinions and value them, whether I ultimately agree or not.

Conclusion—Maintain Your Humanness

Finally, I have found that the very best leaders have displayed a number of personal characteristics, which infused what they did and how they did it. They had the reputation of treating subordinates fairly and equitably. They realized that fairness and equity create both faith and trust in a leader. They also regularly shared the glory of an institution's achievements and did not try to hoard it all for themselves. They recognize that they did not accomplish their goals operating alone.

Another key attribute is that all seem to have a sense of humor—a strong antidote to the pomposity of the power syndrome. For me, the most significant characteristic of great leaders is that they do not lose their humanness or forget what it was like when they started at the bottom.

Such leaders all display this humane quality. They are tough-minded, but not mean spirited. They truly care about all the people in their institution—not as faceless agglomeration, but individually, with all their uniqueness to be treated with respect and genuine affection for their roles, their dedication, and their loyalty. Whether it is the groundskeeper, a mechanic, a clerk, or the genius information technology expert, they are all appreciated and treasured.

A humane CEO is a revered CEO who becomes the spiritual and inspirational leader throughout the institution. So I will close these reflections with an additional maxim to the other two appearing in some of the essays. "While it is better to be gone and not forgotten, than forgotten but not gone. It is even greater to be remembered and revered than only remembered."

ABOUT THE AUTHOR
AND HIS INSPIRATION

I am one of those lucky people who grew up with a wonderful father. He was completely dedicated to our family. He was strong and protective, and by example, he was a moral compass for my brothers and sisters and me. He taught us a sense of responsibility to our family, our community, and to our country.

I can still picture him—wiry and strong—as one of the most talented bricklayers in our hometown. He was a master with his hands. In my mind, there was nothing that Daddy could not do. I can still hear him patiently helping and teaching on the various construction jobs where I was privileged to work for him. He was a hard taskmaster who would not accept anything but excellent work. I can still remember the pride and unconditional love he showered on me and all my siblings as we made our way through childhood.

Despite the wonderful skills of my mother, and the love that she showered on all of us, it is not hard to imagine the difficulties my siblings and I might have had growing up if we had not had both the example of my father, and the stability he brought to our family. And yet many American children are being raised without such stability, without fathers. Many American women are having to shoulder the emotional and financial responsibilities of parenthood alone. Many communities are finding themselves with fewer good male role models to hold up as ideals for their sons; and too many men are living their lives without ever experiencing the joys of fatherhood.

My father was a very special person. What I am today was largely the result of how he influenced and shaped me as his first son. When I am asked today who was the most significant role model in my life, the immediate answer is my father. Oh yes, my life has been touched by presidents of the nation; by business heads of Fortune 100 firms; by pastors and religious leaders of world renown; by presidents and chancellors of leading college and universities. Yet none of them overshadow the place of my father—Wright Lowenstein Lassiter Sr.—in my life and on me.

Daddy taught me two little words when I was very young. The words were *work hard*! My personal and professional life has been built around those two little words. Two words that I have passed on to my son and my daughter. Two powerful words that defined what success I may have experienced.

Because I saw firsthand how my father literally threw himself into everything that he encountered, I wanted to be just like him. I always wanted to show Daddy that I had learned the lessons that he sought to impart in his unique way into my life.

I saw my father experience success in a number of ways. Long before the term *continuing education* was coined, I can remember him and two of his friends who traveled from Vicksburg to Tallulah, Louisiana, to attend night school and earn what is now known as the GED. Later, he attended the Mississippi Baptist Seminary where he earned his undergraduate and graduate degrees in religion and theology. Later, he was a board member of the seminary and a faculty member. Even later, he was awarded an honorary doctoral degree by the seminary.

Because of him, and his example, I have always wanted to be successful. I learned early in my life the relationship between hard work, preparation, and success. Working hard does not always guarantee success, but success is only achieved by hard work and earnest preparation. I have put in my fair share of effort, yet when I take a step back and look at where I am today, I see the fingerprints and footprints of my beloved father.

Let me quickly add that hard work isn't the only component of success; you have to be willing to take risks. In a way, taking risks is even harder than making diligent efforts. Risk introduces the possibility of failure, which is a frightening roadblock on the path to success and responsible living. Through precept and deed, my father taught me how to combine hard work, risk-taking, daring, and courage into a coordinated pattern.

So the time came in my life that I felt this burden to try and capture through the medium of the printed word expressions that reflect and manifest the lessons that I learned from my father. Hopefully, that which is contained in this book and the others that I have written may prove to have some utility for others. Perhaps the readers can discern how proud I am to carry the name of my father.

That has been the inspiration of this author.